THE
TRAMWAYS
OF
EAST ANGLIA

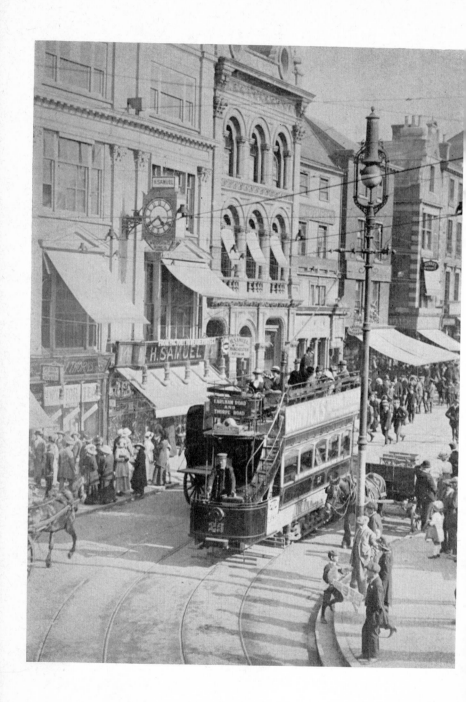

The Tramways
of
East Anglia

by

R. C. Anderson, A.M.Inst.T.

Assistant Traffic Manager,
The Western and Southern National Omnibus Companies

Published in London by
THE LIGHT RAILWAY TRANSPORT LEAGUE
1969

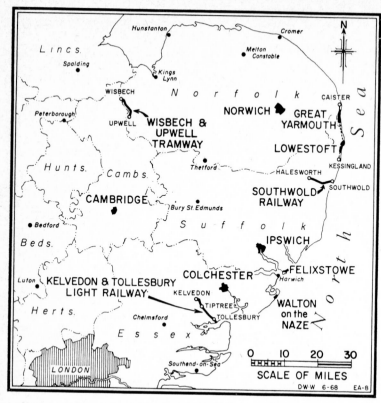

The map above shows the location of the urban tramway systems
described in this book, together with the pier tramways, Wisbech and
Upwell tramway, and light railways.

———

Frontispiece: The open-top double decker was characteristic of East
Anglia's tramways, the atmosphere of which is epitomised in this
animated scene at the junction of The Walk and Guildhall Hill in
Norwich.   *Photo: Neal's of Norwich*

———

Printed by W. J. Fowler & Son (Cricklewood) Ltd.,
Bletchley, Bucks—E6291

© R. C. Anderson
SBN: 900433 00 0

CONTENTS

MAPS

AUTHOR'S ACKNOWLEDGEMENTS

A BOOK of this kind is a co-operative project in that it depends to a large extent on the willingness of many people to assist, by loaning notes or other material from their collections, answering specific questions, or by reading the draft manuscript and improving the contents from their own knowledge. Without this help the book would not have been written, and my grateful thanks go to all those persons who have helped, in particular to W. H. Bett, R. W. Brimblecombe, R. S. Cox, C. Carter, A. B. Dennis, J. C. Gillham, D. Mackley, J. H. Price and R. B. Parr; the general managers of the municipal transport undertakings at Colchester, Great Yarmouth, Ipswich and Lowestoft; the Essex county archivist; the East Suffolk county librarian; the Norwich and Ipswich public libraries; the clerk to the urban district council of Frinton and Walton; and D. W. Willoughby for re-drawing my maps for publication. Last—but certainly not least— to G. B. Claydon, J. Joyce, and the members of the Light Railway Transport League Publications Committee.

R. C. Anderson
Exeter, Devon

The author gratefully acknowledges the permission given to reproduce the photographs used to illustrate this history. Where the name of the owner of the copyright is known, this has been included in the relative caption. The precise origin of many of the illustrations is not known to the author, who wishes to place on record his thanks to these unknown persons who, by their efforts, recorded the early days of the tramways. Several of these prints have come from the author's own collection and from those of A. V. Bird, J. H. Price and W. E. Deamer. I trust that I have not failed to mention any contributor; if I have it is not intentional and I trust my apologies will be accepted.

INTRODUCTION

A S an area, East Anglia is predominantly rural and, excluding the
Wisbech and Upwell steam tramway, the general picture is
of tramways within towns with no interurban linking. In the southern
half of East Anglia, the two electric tramway undertakings at Colchester and Ipswich were municipally promoted, owned and operated.
The undertaking at Lowestoft was privately promoted but the powers
were taken over by the municipality which constructed, owned and
operated the system. The Norwich tramway system was company-
promoted, owned and operated. There had, of course, been several
private schemes for tramways in both areas, and indeed horse tramways had been privately operated at Great Yarmouth, Ipswich and
Cambridge, although in the case of the last-mentioned system, this
was never electrified and became the first tramway abandonment in
the area when the tramways were replaced by "Ortona" buses. The
southern half possessed the only trolleybus system in East Anglia—at
Ipswich—although trolleybuses were discussed and proposed at other
towns.

Today East Anglia is still a rural area, but it was much more so
in the early part of this century, although the coastal towns were busy
with shipping and holidaymakers, giving rise to a need for public street
transport. The transport systems in the area were most varied, ranging
from coastal steamship services through different forms of street transport to mainline rail services. East Anglia is undoubtedly still one of
the unspoilt parts of the British Isles, but from the transport student's
point of view, the period just before the 1914–18 war must have been
among the area's most interesting years. It is hoped, therefore, that
this book will go some way to recording the history of transport in
the area.

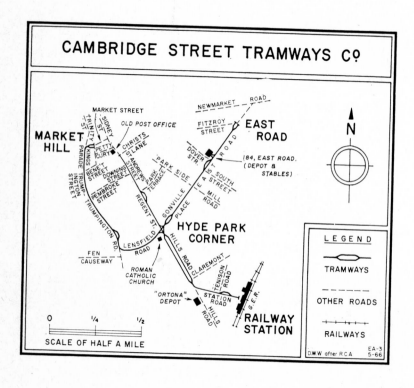

CAMBRIDGE STREET TRAMWAYS Cº

MARKET STREET
OLD POST OFFICE
MARKET HILL
CHRISTS ST LANE
TRINITY ST
SIDNEY ST
PETTY CURY
KINGS PARADE
BENE'T STREET
DOWNING STREET
PEMBROKE STREET
ANDREWS STREET
REGENT ST
TRUMPINGTON ROAD
TRUMPINGTON STREET
PARK TERRACE
PARK SIDE
GONVILLE PLACE
LENSFIELD ROAD
HILLS ROAD
FEN CAUSEWAY

NEWMARKET ROAD
FITZROY STREET
EAST ROAD
EAST ROAD
DOVER STR
SOUTH STREET
MILL ROAD
184, EAST ROAD.
(DEPOT & STABLES)

HYDE PARK CORNER

ROMAN CATHOLIC CHURCH
"ORTONA" DEPOT
CLAREMONT
TENISON ROAD
STATION ROAD
HILLS ROAD
G.E.R.
RAILWAY STATION

N

LEGEND
TRAMWAYS
OTHER ROADS
RAILWAYS

0   ¼   ½
SCALE OF HALF A MILE

D.W.W. after R.C.A

EA-3
5-66

CHAPTER ONE

CAMBRIDGE

EVEN today, Cambridge preserves to a certain extent the atmosphere of a country town, and the only modern industries established before the end of the nineteenth century were a jam-making factory set up in 1873 and a scientific instrument works in 1881. A need for some form of public transport arose from the movement of persons between the various colleges of the university, and this was complemented by the requirements of the expanding population.

Pre-1900

In 1879 the Cambridge Street Tramways Company was formed with a capital of £20,000 in £10 shares (at a later date an amount of £1,200 was added in 4 per cent mortgage debentures) and the object, as stated in the company's prospectus, to:

> "lay down, maintain and work an efficient system of tramways between the town of Cambridge and the Cambridge Station of the Great Eastern, Great Northern, Midland, and London and North Western Railways."

Agreement was reached with the town council over the proposals in respect of the tramways, and the plans were deposited on 30th November, 1878. This original scheme contained a proposal for a track gauge of 3 ft. 6 in., but this was changed to 4 ft. before construction began.

On 21st July, 1879, the Bill received the Royal Assent and the resulting Act was known as the Cambridge Street Tramways Act. Accordingly construction was commenced under the direction of J. F. Meston, the appointed contractor, and by 18th September, 1879, the tramway company's engineer was able to report to his board of directors that the work of laying the tramways was rapidly reaching completion. The trackwork consisted of steel girder rails (5½ in. deep, with a flange width of 5 in., and weighing 71 lb. per yard) laid on a 6-in. bed of concrete. The gauge of 4 ft. was maintained by spiking the rails with dog spikes to transverse sleepers. The paving on the outside and inside of the rails was laid in a serrated form for a width of 6 in., using granite setts ; the remaining portion was laid with tarred macadam. The cost of laying the rails was estimated at £3,617 per mile. Unfortunately, there was some difficulty in finding and acquiring a suitable site for the erection of a depôt and stables, but eventually a plot of land adjacent to East Road was purchased and the buildings were erected here. The address was 184, East Road, Cambridge, and it was here that the tramway company's registered office was situated.

Towards the end of October, 1880, Major-General Hutchinson, R.E., of the Board of Trade, together with Mr. Floyd, C.E., the engineer of the tramways company, inspected the tramways. Major-General Hutchinson expressed his satisfaction with the line, which he passed as fit for public service.

The tramways were opened for traffic on the first completed section from the railway station to the post office (Christ's College) on 27th October, 1880. Six tramway cars, each drawn by one horse, were available for service at the opening (see schedule of cars).

In 1880, the "Cambridge Street Tramways Extensions Provisional Order" was passed. This authorised the company to construct a tramway from a point in Newmarket Road via East Road, Hyde Park Corner, and Trumpington Road, to Market Hill. In the event, the tramway was terminated at Fitzroy Street and the authorised continuation into Newmarket Road was not constructed. (It would seem, therefore, that the depôt and stables had not been constructed in time for the opening of the tramways.)

Late in 1880 there were letters to the editor of the 'Cambridge Chronicle and Independent Press' to the effect that two horses should be used to draw each car in view of the alleged instances of heavy loading. The company tried the two-horse arrangement but later reverted to the practice of one horse per car. There were no gradients of note on any of the roads in which the tramways were laid ; in fact, the difference in levels over the whole system was no more than 10 ft.

The East Road and Trumpington Street tramways (note that the latter was opened in two sections, at first to the Senate House and later to Market Hill) were opened, it is believed, in November, 1880, from Hyde Park Corner to Market Hill and to East Road (Fitzroy Street). This completed the system of tramways in Cambridge. Incidentally, Trumpington Street was restricted to the use of single-deck cars.

10

The tramways were generally of single track with passing places, except that there was approximately a quarter of a mile of double-track tramway from Hyde Park Corner along Hills Road to the junction of Claremont Road, at which point the track became single again before turning into Station Road, along which the tramway was again laid as a single track. The only complicated junction was at Hyde Park Corner. In all, 2.67 (0.67 single and 2.00 double) route miles were laid.

Single-deck car No. 2 of the Cambridge Street Tramways Company on the route between the station and the Post Office. Note the state of the roadway!

The service from the post office via Hyde Park Corner to the railway station operated (in 1900) every 15 minutes from 8 a.m. to 9 a.m., then every 10 minutes throughout the day (seven minutes at the midday and evening peak periods) until 8.35 p.m., with last cars from the post office at 8.50 p.m. and 9.5 p.m. which returned from the station after meeting the 9.18 Great Northern and 9.32 Great Eastern trains from London. On Saturdays, the seven-minute service applied for most of the day. The other service, from Market Hill via Hyde Park Corner to East Road (Workmen's Hall), commenced somewhat later and ran only every 20 minutes. Neither service operated on Sundays.

Fares on both routes were 2d. all the way and 1d. to or from Hyde Park Corner. Books of 1d. (white) and 2d. (green) tickets could be purchased from conductors at a small discount and season tickets were available at 6s. for one month, 15s. for three months, 28s. for six months, and 50s. for a year.

With regard to the conveyance of freight, the company was authorised as follows:

Small animals and poultry were charged ½d. per mile per head; under the 1879 Act, the company could carry freight of all kinds, though there is no evidence that this was ever done or that any freight cars were obtained.

In 1881, 1882 and 1883, a dividend of 5 per cent was paid, but during these three years the company had the benefit of a guarantee from the contractors. Between 1883 and 1896, however, the dividend fluctuated between 2 per cent and 5 per cent. As a result of operating experience, two additional double-deck cars were purchased during the 1880s, but, unfortunately, the exact date appears to be unknown.

Under the Cambridge Street Tramways Act, 1879, there was a clause regarding the company's liability to repair the highways in which the rails were laid, but in 1892 the Corporation agreed to take over the liability from the company, subject to the company paying an annual sum of £325 by quarterly payment. During 1894 another double-deck car was added to the fleet.

The year 1896 saw the introduction of horse buses into Cambridge and this resulted in a considerable loss of revenue to the Cambridge Street Tramways Company, but matters improved when in 1898 the British Electric Traction Co. Ltd. entered into a conditional agreement for the purchase of the shares of the tramways company, and Mr. Emile Garcke joined the Board. However, it was the horse bus operators who went into liquidation in 1900, not the tramways company. Another horse bus service was commenced shortly afterwards, but this suffered the same fate as the first one.

1900–1914

In 1900 the British Electric Traction Co. Ltd. purchased shares in the Cambridge Street Tramways Company and opened negotiations with the Corporation for an extension of tenure and a £60,000 scheme for electrification of the horse tramway. At about the same time the Cambridge town council proposed a Bill to give them powers to purchase the horse tramways and electrify them; it was proposed spending about three-quarters of a million pounds for tramways and waterworks.

Apparently there was failure to reach agreement, as by 1902 Garcke had left the Board and it was evident the British Electric Traction Co. Ltd. had sold their interests in the company when on 12th January, 1904, the Cambridge Electric Tramways Syndicate Ltd. decided to:

"... adopt an Agreement with the British Electric Traction Company Limited for the acquisition of its interest in an Agreement dated 21st June, 1898, between the Cambridge Street Tramways Company of the one part, and the first-named Company of the other part, and for the purchase by this Company of certain shares held by the British Electric Traction Company Limited in the Cambridge Street Tramways Company; and to construct, acquire, equip, maintain, and work by electricity or other power any tramway or tramways in the town or county of Cambridge, and to carry on the business of railway and omnibus proprietors, carriers of passengers and goods, etc."

In 1904 the company operated five double-deck and two single-deck horse cars and twenty-eight horses, employing fourteen drivers and conductors and three horse keepers. A dividend of 3½ per cent had been paid in 1900; 4 per cent in 1901 and 1902. The registered office was now located at 5, Alexandra Road, Cambridge; the company's stables in John Street had been disposed of together with the omnibuses, to pay off four mortgage bonds amounting to £400.

Traffic receipts and passengers carried in those initial years were:

1899 — 882,971 passengers; receipts £3,661
1900 — 857,828 passengers; receipts £3,552
1901 — 815,735 passengers; receipts £3,473
1902 — 851,007 passengers; receipts £3,726
1903 — 752,939 passengers; receipts £3,136

The conclusion is reached that the reasons that prompted the B.E.T. to abandon their scheme for electrification must have similarly affected the C.E.T.S., as this company was wound up between 1910 and 1912. (It is the author's own opinion—obviously open to correction— that the protracted negotiations gave the bus operators such a hold on services in Cambridge that in the end it became apparent that the financial success of a tramway undertaking was open to doubt.)

In 1905, motor bus operation was commenced in Cambridge by a company known as the Cambridge Light Blues, which was joined shortly afterwards by another company known as the Cambridge Motor Omnibus Company. This resulted in severe competition between the tramways company and the two bus companies, mainly on the post office–railway station service. The fight was a severe one, and the "Light Blues" dropped out after six months (it is believed that a conductor put his head out of a vehicle, struck it on an upright and was fatally injured, and that the resulting litigation costs put the company out of business), to be followed shortly afterwards by the Cambridge Omnibus Company Limited, which went into liquidation. Apparently, the company's double-deck vehicles had swept down lamp posts and caused other damage, as a result of which the town council refused to licence the vehicles.

In 1907, J. B. Walford bought up the old Cambridge Motor Omnibus Company and formed the Ortona Motor Company, which commenced operating a service from the post office to the railway station using one Maudslay and three Scott-Stirling single-deck vehicles. After about a year's running between the post office and the railway station, the company secured permission to introduce double-deck buses, which commenced operating through the town to Chesterton. After this the services were considerably developed with much success.

Double-deck car, rebuilt from single decker No. 2, passes an Ortona motor bus in Cambridge.

The Ortona Motor Co. Ltd. had been registered on 28th March, 1908, to take over the business formerly carried on by J. B. Walford. The registered office was at 112, Hills Road, Cambridge, the present local depôt of the Eastern Counties Omnibus Co. Ltd.

During 1909–10, the eighth and final car was purchased by the tramways company.

The further expansion of the Ortona Motor Co. Ltd. had an extremely adverse effect on the number of passengers carried by the Cambridge Street Tramways Company and, consequently, their revenue was reduced. As a result, in 1912, the tramways company defaulted in its quarterly payments to the Corporation in respect of the maintenance

14

of the highway as provided for in the 1892 agreement (see above). The tramways company felt that it had a grievance to the effect that the Corporation had licensed the motor buses which had reduced the company's receipts and it was suggested that it was inequitable that the company should be wound up in respect of this debt to keep up the highway while the bus operators paid nothing.

As a result, on 6th January, 1914, the petition, by the Mayor and Corporation of Cambridge, for the compulsory winding-up of the Cambridge Street Tramways Company was heard before Mr. Justice Astbury in the Chancery Division of the High Court.

Apparently, the attention of Parliament had been called to the grievance, but Mr. Justice Astbury said that he could not very well keep the petition in suspense until Parliament made up its mind as to the respective portions of the highway upkeep to be borne by the tramways company and the motor bus operators. If he could have seen that the difficulties of the tramways company were only temporary, the matter might have been different, but the sum due was steadily mounting up as each quarter's dues remained unpaid, and the position of the tramways company became correspondingly worse. An order for the compulsory winding-up was therefore made.

However, the tramways continued for a further four weeks, and it was not until early in February, 1914, that a notice was posted in the cars informing the public that the tramways would cease to operate on Wednesday, 18th February, 1914. On the last day, local residents took the opportunity to have a final ride on the cars which had served

The last car in Cambridge; a specially-posed photograph outside the depôt.

15

Cambridge for 34 years; once again, for a short time, the tramways company's services were well patronised. The official last car left the railway station at 6.25 p.m., driven by Ephraim Skinner, the company's oldest driver.

On Friday, 20th February, 1914, an auction was held at the company's depôt in East Road. It was attended by about 600 people and, besides the tramway cars and horses, such items as "nine leather cash bags," "eight drivers' leather caps," and a "quantity of tram tickets" fetched good prices as souvenirs. The amounts paid for the cars varied from £7 15s. for a single-deck car to £15 for a double-deck car. The horses fetched from 14½ gn. for a ten-year-old brown horse to 40½ gn. for a seven-year-old bay horse. (Most of the prices were in the 20-30 gn. range, which showed a considerable increase in the prices paid for the horses sold when the Yarmouth and Gorleston Tramway Company was closed.)

On the same day as the auction took place, the Ortona Motor Co. Ltd. received licences from the Cambridge Town Council Watch Committee for six more buses, to meet the increased traffic arising from the closing of the tramways.

The depôt was taken over in 1914 by V. Prior, who used it as a fish market until 1928, when it was used by a corn chandler until 1938. In that year a motor engineering business moved into the premises in place of the corn chandler, and the building was used for motor engineering until 1944. Since 1944, Peaks Furniture Depository have been the occupiers of the old tramway depôt.

Schedule of cars

The first six cars (numbered 1-6) were delivered for the opening of the tramway and were listed as two double-deck cars, two single-deck cars, and two cars with "a partition for luggage." The double-deck cars were described as "well-built wood and iron cars, well lighted at sides, front and back, well-decorated wood backs to seats inside, and loose plush-covered cushions; sliding doors at back and front, lamps and brakes at each end; seating accommodation for 18 inside and 23 outside [*although this varied between cars*]; dimensions 21 ft. 8 in. by 6 ft. 1 in. by 10 ft. 9 in. high." The cars cost £300 each and were built by the Starbuck Car and Wagon Co. Ltd., Birkenhead.

No. 1. Double-deck, with round dashes and seven windows per side. All photographs of this car show garden seats, although it is extremely doubtful whether these were of 1880 vintage and more likely they replaced knifeboard seating as a result of experience gained with No. 7. Seating was for 18 inside and 23 outside. This car was sold on 20th February, 1914, the day of the auction, to a Mr. Hunt of Coton, for £10.

No. 2. Originally a single-deck car with flat dashes and seven windows per side, it was later converted to a double-decker with knifeboard seating for 24 outside and 18 inside.

No. 3. Originally a single-deck car. An early photograph of this car, taken in 1882, shows round dashes and a half canopy, at least at one end, as though it had been delivered unfinished by Starbuck. The roof then was very much of the knifeboard style, the body only needing seats and a pair of staircases to convert it into a double-decker. A note of the half-yearly meeting in October, 1900, mentions that "the Directors wish to place another car with top seats into service," which suggests that either No. 2 or No. 3 had already been converted by that date. (It is likely to have been No. 3, as there was so little work necessary for such a conversion.) No. 3 had six windows per side and seats for 18 inside and 22 outside. Nos. 2 and 3 were sold to a Mr. Hudson for £8 10s. each.

No. 4. This car was identical to No. 3, but was delivered as a complete double-deck car with knifeboard seating for 22 and interior seating for 18. The car had round dashes and six windows per side. It was sold on 20th February, 1914, to a Mr. Speechly, slaughterer, of Newmarket Road, Cambridge, for £8 15s.

Nos. 5 and 6. Saloons with five windows per side. In the saloon there was a partition situated in line with the third pair of window pillars. The reason was that these cars were planned for use on the station route to carry in the smaller "room" the luggage of students and others, but after about 11 years they were apparently so little used in this way that it was reported in March, 1892, that the partitions were in the process of being removed. The cars had almost flat dashes, with a small bulge in the centre of the body, which had a seating capacity for 18. These two cars provided a 20-minute service on the East Road route at a speed of 5 miles per hour. No. 5 was sold to a Mr. Pamplin and No. 6 to a Mr. Wright of Haddenham, both for £7 15s.

No. 7. Purchased in the first half of 1894 and apparently similar to No. 1, this car, which had seats for 18 inside and 23 on garden seats outside, was sold to a Mr. Howard for £9 15s.

B

No. 8. The last car to be purchased in 1909/10, this double-decker had five windows per side and seated 18 inside and 22 outside on garden seats. It was sold to a Major Whitmore for £15.

Livery was red waist panels lined out in gold, with a small fleet number surrounded by a band located centrally on the waist panel; cream rocker panels, corner pillars and ventilator boards, lined out in black. The wording "CAMBRIDGE STREET TRAMWAYS" was displayed full length in shaded gold in the rocker panel. On the dashes (red or cream, it depended on the car, but it appears that double-deck cars had red dashes, and single-deck cars had cream dashes), the fleet number was displayed in large numerals. Advertisement boards were carried on both single-deck and double-deck cars; destination boards were carried in holders fitted midway between the upper window rail and the cant rail.

Specimen ticket of the Cambridge tramways.

CHAPTER TWO

COLCHESTER

SITUATED on the River Colne, Colchester—the Roman Camulo-dunum, and the oldest recorded town in Great Britain—possesses an eleventh-century castle with the largest Norman keep in England. Famous for its oysters, Colchester was sufficiently close to London to be attractive for industrial development.

Perhaps one of the most important dates in the development of modern Colchester was 29th March, 1843, because it was on this day that the Eastern Counties Railway officially opened their railway from Shoreditch to Colchester.

At this time, the population of Colchester was about 18,000 persons, with the heaviest concentration of population in the St. Botolph's area and to the south-east of this point. The population was further increased by the establishment between 1854 and 1856 of military camps, and in 1870 by building development in the south-east of the town and along the Lexden Road, which had hitherto separated the village of Lexden from Colchester.

Industrial development got underway in 1865, when Messrs. Davey, Paxman & Co. started making steam engines and agricultural machinery at premises, first in High Street, then Culver Street and, by 1876, at the Standard Iron Works, Hythe.

Additional railways had been established, first by the Great Eastern Railway which, in 1862, opened railways from Marks Tey up the Colne Valley and from Manningtree to Harwich, and second by the Tendring Hundred Railway which opened a line to St. Botolph's station in 1867. Improvements to the river carried out under Acts of 1847, 1865 and 1882, resulted in better facilities for barges, but did not make a deep water port.

The first proposal to construct and work a street tramway in Colchester came in 1883. As a result of this proposal, a Bill was presented in Parliament to work a steam tramway, and a Provisional Order was obtained. Track laying was commenced between North Station and High Street and had reached Middleborough when financial difficulties caused the company to collapse, thereby resulting in the scheme falling through. Apparently the track and other materials were forfeited to Colchester Corporation, who removed the track in North Station Road.

No further developments came until 1898 (the same year in which the power station in Osborne Road was opened), when the British Electric Traction Company applied for a Light Railway Order to permit them to introduce a system of electric tramways into the borough on five short routes radiating from the town centre. In addition, the British Electric Traction Company sought compulsory powers to purchase and then demolish a few houses in order to widen a narrow section of road. However, the Light Railway Commissioners rejected the application on 15th August, 1899, on the grounds that, as the proposed system of tramways was wholly within the borough, it was an urban tramway and should have been promoted under the Tramways Act, 1870. Subsequently, the Light Railway Commissioners did authorise a number of urban tramways under the Light Railways Act, 1896—Southend-on-Sea and Lowestoft, for instance.

About this time, municipal interest in public street transport became more positive, and several different schemes were proposed. These included a most intriguing scheme which, in August, 1901, drew from the Board of Trade a reply to the effect that the Colchester town council's proposal to run cars or omnibuses by overhead electric wires, without laying rails, could not be authorised under the Tramways Act, 1870. But for this setback, Colchester might have become Britain's first trolleybus operator, presumably using one of the systems then being tried in Germany. Consequently, in 1901, the Corporation presented to Parliament a Bill which resulted in an Act of 1901 authorising the Colchester Corporation to construct and work a system of 3 ft. 6in. gauge electric tramways within the borough.

In November, 1901, the Railways and General Construction and Maintenance Co. Ltd. applied to the Light Railway Commissioners for a Southend and Colchester Light Railway. This light railway was proposed to link with the Colchester Corporation system at a terminal point which would have been at the junction of the present B1026 road and the Colchester Corporation borough boundary. From this point, the promoters no doubt hoped to receive running powers into Colchester proper over the Colchester Corporation system, but as the track gauge of the proposed light railway was 4 ft. 8½ in., and the Corporation's proposed track gauge was 3ft. 6 in., one wonders what compromise would have resulted. However, despite the fact that the

Southend and Colchester Light Railway eventually got certain modified powers (their first proposals were rejected at a public enquiry on 8th May, 1902), no construction was undertaken.

In February, 1903, the Colchester town council adopted by 18 votes to 9 an electric tramway scheme at an estimated cost of £63,414. This apparent repetition of the decision of 1901 is explained by the fact that a section of the council were opposed to the scheme and wished to wait to see how the then somewhat unreliable motor bus would develop before deciding in favour of electric tramways.

Early in 1904, the rails were delivered to Colchester from Belgium, and construction of both track and overhead line equipment was carried out by the contractors, J. G. White & Co. Ltd. Messrs. Lacey and Sillar were the engineers. The overhead suspension was of various types; centre poles were erected in High Street, and side poles with bracket arms or span wires were used at other places according to the width of road. Power for working the tramways was taken from the Corporation's own electricity works, which was slightly enlarged for the opening of the tramways. The routes constructed consisted of 5 miles 11 chains of route, 1 mile 77 chains of which were double track, and were as follows:

North Station to Lexden (Straight Road Junction)
North Station to East Gates
North Station to Hythe (Quay)

At the North Station it was necessary for the roadway to be lowered to permit the passage of the cars. The steepest gradient was 1 in 12 and the sharpest curve had a radius of 40 feet. In view of the fact that track brakes had to be fitted when there was an appreciable distance at a gradient steeper than 1 in 15 the Colchester cars were fitted with Newell track brakes. The depôt was, and still is, in Magdalen Street on the Hythe route.

The total cost of the tramway scheme was about £65,000; loans received were as follows:

12th December, 1901 — £2,250 for 30 years.
11th June, 1903 — £60,895 for 24 years.

On 28th July, 1904, the tramway system was opened to the public with great ceremony when, in pouring rain, the Mayoress drove the first car (No. 13) from the Town Hall to Lexden, then to North Station and back to the Town Hall. Despite the rain a large crowd was present at the opening ceremony when car No. 13, gaily decked out with flags and bunting and conveying invited guests, led the procession of four cars. Sixteen cars, Nos. 1–16, were delivered and available at the opening date to work the services, which were operated from the North Station to each of the three termini. There was a service at a 15-minute frequency on each leg, combining to give a five-minute frequency between High Street and North Station. First cars started at 5 a.m. on weekdays and 9 a.m. on Sundays, and the services continued until 11 p.m.

On 3rd August, 1904, Colchester Corporation received a deputation of clergymen and ministers who requested that there should be a restriction on the running of services on the tramways during Divine Service on Sundays. After a sharp debate it was decided by a small majority not to make any alterations whatever.

Specimen fares at the opening of the tramways were:

North Station–Top North Hill	1d.
Top North Hill–Holly Lodge	1d.
Holly Lodge–Straight Road	1d.
East Gates–High Street	1d.
Hythe–High Street	1d.

The opening of the Colchester electric tramways, 28th July, 1904. The scene in the High Street, with the Town Hall and the New Theatre.

No. 13, the inaugural car, driven by the Mayoress at the formal opening of the tramways.

In 1905, the Corporation obtained a further Act of Parliament which authorised them to make the only extension which was made to the original tramways. This extension, opened on 28th January, 1906, was of 22 chains double and 25 chains single track from St. Botolph's to the Recreation Ground. The service introduced to work over this extension was from the North Station to the Recreation Ground. To cover the cost of constructing this extension and providing two additional cars (Nos. 17 and 18 delivered in July, 1906) to work the additional service, a loan of £6,410 was obtained on 25th September, 1905, repayable over a period of 27 years.

This extension brought the route mileage up to a total of 5 miles 39.34 chains (3 miles 43.5 chains single track and 2 miles 15.84 chains double track).

Routes described

As all four services traversed North Hill and three traversed High Street, the track was laid double to the George Hotel, from which point the track was laid single to the top of Queen Street, where the routes diverged, the East Gate route continuing as single track in East Hill to its terminus.

Double track was laid in Queen Street to the point at which the Hythe and Recreation Ground routes separated; from here on each route continued as single track. The Lexden route was laid double

23

in Head Street and around the corner into Crouch Street, and thence as single track to its terminus at Lexden (Straight Road). At the junction of High Street and Head Street there was a double-track triangular junction.

A crossover was provided in High Street, near the Town Hall, and was used by cars on short workings. To prevent cars from meeting on the single track laid in the north end of Queen Street (where the road curved) to the junction with High Street, a signalling system was installed. At each end of the section there was a signal light which was switched on by the driver of a car entering the section ; as the car left the section it was necessary for the driver to switch the lights off again.

During the closing months of 1908, a car caught the handle of a barrel organ in St. Botolph's Street and turned it over, with the result that the blind organist sued the Corporation for £14 15s. They in turn alleged obstruction. The matter was finally settled out of court without the Corporation admitting liability.

Service numbers were not used ; the car's destination was displayed by means of an illuminated destination indicator box set high above the front top deck rails. On each side of the car along the waist rail there was also a destination board which always displayed the car's outer terminus whichever direction the car was proceeding. Towards the end of 1913 return fares were introduced on the North Hill–Recreation Ground service and on the North Hill–Walpole Road section of the North Hill– Hythe service.

The tramways had an uneventful life, although they naturally shared, in common with other tramway undertakings, the difficulties caused by the 1914–1918 war. The track became progressively worse, and no modernisation work was undertaken on any of the cars at all during their life. In 1925, W. H. Soulby succeeded R. R. C. Bullough who had been General Manager of the tramways since they opened in 1904.

The fares charged on the tramways at this time were 1d., 1½d., 2d., 2½d. and 3d., according to distance, the through fare on each route being 3d. except for North Station to East Gates which was 2½d. From the town centre, fares were 2d. to North Station, Hythe or the Recreation Ground, and 1d. or 1½d. for shorter journeys.

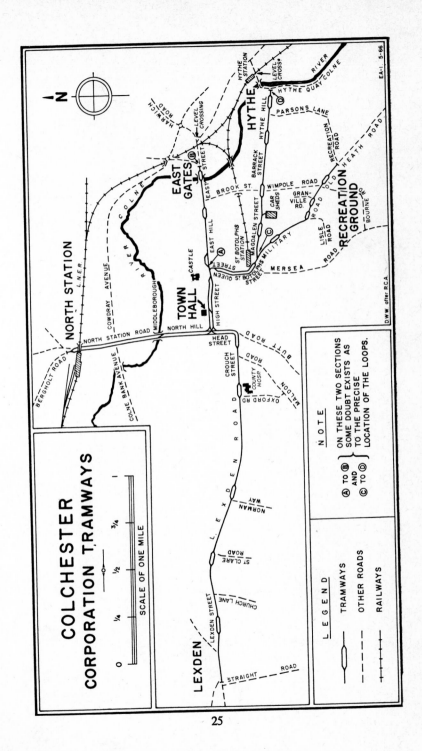

COLCHESTER
CORPORATION TRAMWAYS

SCALE OF ONE MILE

0   ¼   ½   ¾   1

N

NORTH STATION

LEXDEN

TOWN HALL

EAST GATES

HYTHE

RECREATION GROUND

HARWICH ROAD
LEVEL CROSSING
LEVEL CROSS
HYTHE STATION
HYTHE HILL
HYTHE QUAY
RIVER COLNE
PARSONS LANE
BARRACK STREET
RECREATION ROAD
HEATH ROAD
BROOK ST.
WIMPOLE ROAD
EAST STREET
MAGDALEN STREET
CAR SHEDS
GRANVILLE RD.
OLD HEATH ROAD
BOURNE ROAD
LISLE ROAD
EAST HILL
ST BOTOLPHS STATION
CASTLE
ST BOTOLPHS STREET QUEEN STREET
MILITARY ROAD
MERSEA ROAD
RIVER COLNE
COWDRAY AVENUE
LNER
MIDDLEBOROUGH
NORTH HILL
HIGH STREET
NORTH STATION ROAD
BERGHOLT ROAD
COLNE BANK AVENUE
HEAD STREET
CROUCH STREET
COUNTY HOSP.
OXFORD RD.
BUTT ROAD
MALDON ROAD
LEXDEN ROAD
NORMAN WAY
ST CLARE ROAD
CHURCH LANE
LEXDEN STREET
STRAIGHT ROAD

EA-1. 5-66
D.W.W. after R.C.A.

LEGEND

TRAMWAYS
OTHER ROADS
RAILWAYS

NOTE

ⓐ TO Ⓑ
AND
Ⓒ TO Ⓓ
ON THESE TWO SECTIONS SOME DOUBT EXISTS AS TO THE PRECISE LOCATION OF THE LOOPS.

Colchester car No. 10 decorated for the conveyance of a wedding party.

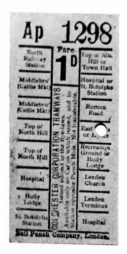

Specimen tickets of Colchester Corporation Tramways.

Children over three and under 12 years of age were charged half the adult fare, but no fare was less than 1d. In the case of the fare being 1½d. or 2½d., the half fare was reckoned as 1d. or 1½d.

Children going to and from school between the hours of 8 a.m. and 9.30 a.m., 12 noon and 2.30 p.m., and 3.30 p.m. and 6 p.m. were allowed to travel at the reduced fare of 1d. between Head Street and any terminus.

Workpeople were allowed to travel on Workpeople's Cars denoted on timetables, at 1d. fare between Head Street and any terminus.

Dogs were allowed on top of cars only, at adult passenger fares.

Passengers were entitled to carry by hand in the car personal luggage, not of a bulky nature, up to 28 lb. in weight. All other luggage not exceeding 56 lb. in weight, between Head Street and any terminus, 1d. per package.

In 1927—the year in which the Osborne Road power station was replaced by a new generating station on Hythe Quay—the Colchester town council decided to abandon the tramways and presented a Bill to Parliament which resulted in an Act of 1927 authorising the Corporation to:

    (a) Abandon the tramways.
    (b) Operate motor buses anywhere within the borough.
    (c) Operate trolleybuses on the tramway routes.
    (d) Operate motor buses on the portion of Gosbecks Road which was in the parish of Stanway. This section was later taken into the borough.

Arising from this proposal, the National Omnibus and Transport Company Limited (the particular area then concerned later became the present Eastern National Omnibus Co. Ltd.) offered to operate bus services within the borough of Colchester if the trams were scrapped, making the Corporation a yearly payment of £550. Similar offers were made by two local operators, Blackwell's and Berry's, but the council decided not to accept them but to proceed with their own scheme to replace the tramways by buses. No buses were operated by the Corporation prior to the passing of the 1927 Act. Bus services in and about the borough were, in fact, provided by a number of large and small private operators who charged, over common stages within the borough, fares 50 per cent higher than those charged by the Corporation on the tramways.

The first section of tramway to be replaced by Corporation buses was between High Street and East Gates (the replaced tramway *service* was, of course, North Station–East Gates), when on 21st May, 1928, four Dennis single-deck buses (Nos. 1–4) commenced operating two half-hourly services as follows:

  (a) Parsons Heath–Shrub End (Leather Bottle).
  (b) Greenstead Road (Hythe Station Road)–Drury Hotel.

These four buses were supplemented by two further Dennis single-deckers (Nos. 5 and 6) in May, 1928, and later by another three similar vehicles (Nos. 7–9). The first double-deck buses (Dennis, Nos. 10 and 11) were delivered with Nos. 7–9 in September, 1928, and these vehicles were used to replace the North Station–Lexden tramway service (i.e. the High Street–Lexden section of tramway was abandoned) on 1st October, 1928; the last tram ran on 30th September, 1928. In March, 1929, new bus services were introduced between High Street and Bergholt Road and between High Street and Mile End.

Due to the bad state of the tramway track between the North Station and the top of North Hill, this section was abandoned in the summer of 1929 and the tramway services to Hythe and the Recreation Ground commenced from the top of North Hill, where a crossover was already laid. The recently-introduced bus service provided the facility over the abandoned section of tramway.

Arising from the Corporation's bus operation, the system whereby private bus operators charged 50 per cent over and above the Corporation's tram fares over common stages was replaced on 3rd July, 1929, by an arrangement whereby private bus operators charged the same fares as the Corporation within the borough of Colchester but used Corporation bus tickets for journeys wholly within the borough and paid the Corporation 25 per cent of the receipts. It should be remembered that at this time buses were licensed for services as hackney carriages by the local authorities in whose area they operated, and consequently a bus-operating local authority had a good deal of power in situations where there was competition between Corporation and private bus services.

Two Dennis double-deck buses (Nos. 12 and 14) and one Dennis single-deck bus (No. 13) were delivered early in 1929 and were followed in October, 1929, by two further Dennis single-deckers (Nos. 18 and 19). The North Hill–Recreation Ground tramway service was augmented by a new bus service, introduced between St. Botolph's Station and Old Heath via the Recreation Ground. Another new bus service which was commenced at about the same time was from High Street to Middlewick via Mersea Road. The last Dennis vehicles to be purchased by Colchester Corporation were delivered in December, 1929; they were numbered 15 to 17, were double-deckers, and, like their predecessors, had Strachan and Brown bodies.

On 9th December, 1929, buses finally replaced the trams (which had ceased on 8th December, 1929) on the two remaining services to Hythe and the Recreation Ground. The new bus services were North Station–Recreation Ground and Hythe to Bergholt Road or Mile End.

After abandonment, most of the rails were lifted (some, however, remained in the roadway) and the roads reinstated. This work, together with certain alterations made to the tram depôt, cost £10,000.

The sequel to the question of fares to be charged within the borough by private operators came when Colchester Corporation applied to the newly-formed Traffic Commissioners for a variation of the conditions attached to road service licences in respect of the private operators who competed with the Corporation services, so as to pro-

This view of car No. 4 illustrates the offset trolley standard.

vide that it would be compulsory for the private operators to charge 50 per cent over and above the fares charged at that time on the Corporation buses and in future chargeable for travel upon Corporation buses.

At a public sitting on 27th April, 1932, at the Town Hall, Colchester, at which the case was put to the Traffic Commissioners, the decision was against protective fares for Colchester Corporation and their application was unsuccessful. As a result, private operators and the Corporation have common fares over common stages.

Since abandoning the tramways, Colchester Corporation have expanded their bus services to meet new developments and, consequently, the number of vehicles required for normal traffic purposes is about 38.

Schedule of cars

1–16

Four-wheel open-top cars with three windows per side, balcony top decks, longitudinal wooden seating in the saloon, and reversed staircases. The cars, which were of the "Preston" type, had seating for 22 passengers on the lower deck, 24 passengers outside, were supplied by Dick, Kerr & Co. The bodies, built by the Electric Railway and Tramway Carriage Works Ltd., were mounted on Brill 21E trucks which had 2 x 35 h.p. Dick, Kerr motors, Dick, Kerr controllers, and Newell magnetic brakes. Destination indicators were carried high above the front top deck rails and there were also side destination boards. No side advertisements were carried on the decency screens, but in later years advertisements were carried around the decency screens over the canopy at each end of the car. The trolley standards were set to one side of the car. Each car cost £575.

17–18

Similar to 1–16, supplied 1906, but had direct staircases, and were built by the United Electric Car Co. Ltd.

The cars were finished in a livery of maroon and cream; maroon on trolley standard, edge of roof, canopy surrounds, dashes, stair stringers and waist panels; cream on decency screen, underside of stairs, window pillars and surrounds, and rocker panels. The Colchester Corporation crest was displayed midway on waist panels, the words "COLCHESTER CORPORATION TRAMWAYS" in gold on rocker

Car No. 13 in later years; note the introduction of advertising displays.

panels, which were also lined out in black. Fleet number in gold was displayed on dashes above headlamps. The maroon-painted areas were lined out in gold.

Colchester Corporation Tramways had no works cars, but they did have a horse-drawn tower wagon which, on occasions, was towed by a tramway car. This tower wagon is still in use at the Corporation bus garage.

After the closure of the tramways, the majority of the car bodies were sold to a local builder who used them as site huts. No. 13 survived until 1960 as a potting shed on a site alongside the Harwich Road. Two further cars (Nos. 6 and 9) survived until 1963 as garden sheds in local villages and may still exist.

Schedule of buses purchased to replace the tramways

Fleet No.	Registration No.	Date new	Chassis type	Body builder	Body type & seats	Withdrawn
1	VW 4389	May, 1928	Dennis 'G'	Strachan	B20F	1944
2	VW 4390	"	"	& Brown	"	1944
3	VW 4391	"	"	"	"	1945
4	VW 4392	"	"	"	"	1943
5	VW 5125	June, 1928	Dennis 'E'	"	B31D	1941
6	VW 5126	"	"	"	"	1942
7	VW 6463	Sept., 1928	"	"	B32D	1943
8	VW 6462	"	"	"	B31D	1943
9	VW 6464	"	"	"	"	1943
10	VW 6482	"	Dennis 'H'	"	OH24/24R	1939
11	VW 6481	"	"	"	"	1943
12	VW 8425	May, 1929	"	"	"	1944
13	VW 8426	"	Dennis 'E'	"	B31D	1939
14	VW 8424	"	Dennis 'H'	"	H24/24R	1943
15	VX 3223	Dec., 1929	Dennis 'HS'	"	"	1944
16	VX 3224	"	"	"	"	1945
17	VX 3222	"	"	"	"	1944
18	VX 2746	Oct., 1929	Dennis 'EV'	"	B31D	1945
19	VX 2745	"	"	"	"	1945

B—bus; F—front entrance; OH—open top, normal seating pattern
R—rear entrance; D—dual entrance; H—high bridge

The buses were painted in a livery of tuscan red and cream; the main body panels, bonnet, stairs, etc., were tuscan red; the window pillars, window surrounds and bands immediately below the window rails, and roof domes, were cream; that part of the roof not painted cream was silver. The red panels were lined out in gold, and the fleet name and Corporation crest were displayed on the lower (red) side panels—COLCHESTER (crest) CORPORATION. An exception to this layout was that used for Nos. 1–4; these had the words "COLCHESTER CORPORATION" on the cream waistband and the Corporation crest on the lower (tuscan red) side panels. The cream roof domes and gold lining were discontinued after 1939.

All vehicles had roller blind destination indicators and a short side board on the waistband. In 1933, when service numbers were introduced, the destination indicators were modified to have these fitted.

CHAPTER THREE

GREAT YARMOUTH

Pre-1900

AT the turn of the nineteenth century, Great Yarmouth was the headquarters of the great autumn herring fishing industry and, in the autumn of 1913, there were still a thousand craft fishing out of Yarmouth which, situated at the mouth of the River Yare, made—and still makes—an admirable port. It is not surprising, therefore, when one considers this in the light of the number of persons employed, that Yarmouth should have been earlier on the scene than most East Anglian towns in having public transport for the conveyance of work-people who were mainly engaged in the fishing and ancillary industries.

The very feature which made Yarmouth a port—the mouth of the Yare—was also a major stumbling block to the aspirations of the early tramway men, as it was necessary to cross this stretch of water if one wanted to travel from Yarmouth to Southtown and Gorleston. A narrow wooden bridge, raised and lowered by hand winches, did exist on the site of the present Haven Bridge.

The first proposal to construct a tramway came in 1870, when the East Suffolk Tramway Company proposed a tramway from Southtown railway station via Gorleston, Lowestoft and Southwold to Halesworth, where the tramway was to meet at a junction with the Great Eastern Railway. The proposed motive power is not known.

This scheme was changed somewhat, however, and the East Anglian Tramway Order, 1871, provided for a horse tramway from Southtown railway station to Gorleston. In October, 1871, the first sod was cut by E. A. K. Lacon and the tramway was built under the supervision of Octavius Horne, a London businessman. A gauge of 4ft. 8½ in. was chosen and the rails were laid on wooden sleepers. The tramway was completed early in 1875 and was formally opened on 1st April, 1875, by the Mayor of Yarmouth, R. D. Barber. On the first day of operation the revenue was £20. The service was operated at quarter-hourly intervals, but it could take up to 2½ hours to complete the single journey.

33

c

In April, 1878, the Yarmouth and Gorleston Tramways Company Limited was formed with a share capital of £25,000 in £10 shares and debentures amounting to £5,000 to acquire the original company, which besides the tramway and premises had ten cars and 40 horses.

As a result, in 1882, the tramway was reconstructed with girder rails laid in concrete, this time to a gauge of 3 ft. 6 in. A depôt and stables were erected at a site near to that where the Great Yarmouth Corporation later built their depôt when the horse tramway was municipalised and electrified. The rolling stock consisted of ten 46-seat double-deck cars, with a stud of 68 horses. (The company also operated six double-deck horse buses and one 'station' bus.) Short extensions were made in 1884, 1886, and again in 1898, bringing the route length up to 2 miles and 6 furlongs, and the track length up to 3 miles 2 furlongs and 3.25 chains.

The staff consisted of sixteen drivers and conductors, one foreman, one inspector, four horse-keepers, one car-washer, two granary hands, one saddler, one carpenter, two permanent-way men, and one boy. The company's registered office was at the depôt in Gorleston.

At the Gorleston end of the tramway, the route from the High Street was via Lowestoft Road, England's Lane and Pier Walk, terminating on the quay outside the King William IV public house. This was the summer terminus; the winter terminus was at Feather's Plain. To assist the cars to climb the hill up Lowestoft Road to the corner of England's Lane, a trace horse was attached at Feather's Plain. In the winter months when snow had fallen, the first car was preceded by a snow plough and two horses pulled each service car. The service was operated by ten cars in summer, five cars until Christmas, and four cars until the summer build-up recommenced. Additional cars (in winter) worked between Southtown station and Half Way House.

The early history of the concern was not very encouraging. Six years' working brought a loss of £17,000, and it was then thought wise to write down the capital to £18,000 in £1 shares. In 1883, owing to extensions, the total rose to £20,000. As a result of the reduction in capital, the company was able to pay an average dividend of 5½ per cent per annum.

The Yarmouth and Gorleston Tramways Co. Ltd. obtained powers to conduct and work horse tramways in Lowestoft but nothing came of this proposal. (See Lowestoft Corporation Tramways, chapter 5.)

Horse car of the Yarmouth and Gorleston Tramways Company.

Horse car at Gorleston, Feathers Plain; note the new electric cars in the background, parked outside the depôt. *Photo: Courtesy R. C. H. Fairbairn*

Bus services in Yarmouth were first provided by wagonettes and later by horse buses pulled by two horses. The services operated were from Newtown to Friars Lane via Caister Road, Northgate Street, Market Place and King Street, on a 15-minute frequency at a fare of 2d. During the summer, a service operated at ten-minute intervals between Southtown railway station and the beach via Vauxhall railway station.

Wagonettes were also used to provide a service between Yarmouth and Caister.

One trip per day was operated between the Jetty (Yarmouth) and North Quay in connection with a boat trip to Norwich; the tramway company owned the horse buses and in 1899 had purchased shares in the Yarmouth and Gorleston Steamboat Co. Ltd., at a cost of £8,140, as a result of which cheap trips were operated between Yarmouth and Gorleston, out by tram and return by boat, at a fare of 6d. Incidentally, a horse bus service was operated from the Buck public house, Yarmouth, to Gorleston several times daily.

In 1900, the British Electric Traction Company (B.E.T.) formed the Great Yarmouth and District Tramways Company Limited, acquiring "practically the whole" of the share capital at less than 75 per cent of its par value. It was the intention of the B.E.T. to apply for powers to electrify the horse tramway, but interest in municipal operation of tramways was growing in Yarmouth and the Corporation vetoed each attempt made by the B.E.T. for the necessary powers to electrify the horse tramway.

In 1896, the movement for municipal tramways had begun to be felt, and by 1898 the Corporation had proposed a scheme of tramways for which Parliamentary powers were obtained in 1899. A Tramways Committee, with Alderman Frank Arnold as its chairman, was formed and it was proposed that work on the construction of the proposed tramways should immediately be commenced.

Unfortunately, it was found that, due to the boom in trade, steel rails were costing £10 per ton and it was decided to defer the date of commencing construction until the price of steel had dropped; this may have been the reason for the swing in public feeling which turned towards the idea of constructing the tramways and leasing them to a company to operate. In 1900, as a protest against this idea, Alderman Arnold resigned from the chairmanship of the Tramways Committee and his place as chairman was taken by C. S. Orde, the Deputy Mayor.

1900–1914

Apparently the offers from interested operating companies (among them were the British Electric Traction Company Limited and the

36

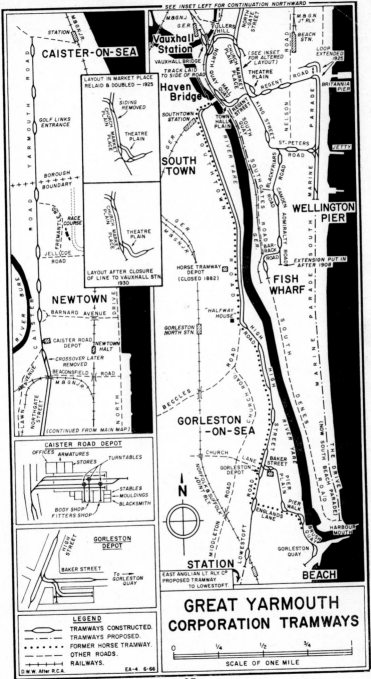

CAISTER-ON-SEA

STATION

M & G N J R

GOLF LINKS
ENTRANCE

BOROUGH
BOUNDARY

FREMANTLE RD

RACE
COURSE

JELLICOE
ROAD

NEWTOWN

BARNARD AVENUE

CAISTER ROAD
DEPOT

NEWTOWN
HALT

CROSSOVER LATER
REMOVED

BEACONSFIELD ROAD

M & G N J R

(CONTINUED FROM MAIN MAP.)

LAYOUT IN MARKET PLACE
RELAID & DOUBLED — 1925

SIDING
REMOVED

CHURCH
MARKET
PLAIN

THEATRE
PLAIN

CHURCH
MARKET
PLAIN

THEATRE
PLAIN

LAYOUT AFTER CLOSURE
OF LINE TO VAUXHALL STN.
1930

M & G N J
G E R
FULLERS
HILL

Vauxhall
Station

VAUXHALL BRIDGE

TRACK LAID
TO SIDE OF ROAD

Haven
Bridge

SOUTHTOWN
STATION

SOUTH
TOWN

HORSE TRAMWAY
DEPOT
(CLOSED 1882)

"HALFWAY
HOUSE"

GORLESTON
NORTH STN.

G E R
M & G N J R

BECCLES ROAD

GORLESTON
-ON-SEA

CHURCH LANE

CHURCH ROAD

GORLESTON
DEPOT

BAKER
STREET

NORFOLK & SUFFOLK
JOINT RLY.

MIDDLETON ROAD

LOWESTOFT ROAD

ENGLANDS
LANE

STATION

EAST ANGLIAN LT. RLY. Cº
PROPOSED TRAMWAY
TO LOWESTOFT

NORTH
GATE
STREET

CHURCH
PLAIN

MARKET
PLACE

NORTH QUAY

HALL QUAY

THEATRE
PLAIN

REGENT ROAD

(SEE INSET FOR ALTERED
LAYOUT)

TOWN
HALL
PLAIN

REGENT
STREET

KING STREET

SOUTH
QUAY

SOUTHGATES ROAD

RIVER YARE

BLACKFRIARS ROAD

CAMDEN ROAD

BAR-
RACK
ROAD

HIGH ROAD

SOUTH DENES ROAD

HIGH ROAD

RIVER YARE

M & G N
JT RLY

BEACH
STN.

LOOP
EXTENDED
1925

BRITANNIA
PIER

ST. PETERS
ROAD

JETTY

WELLINGTON
PIER

ADMIRALTY ROAD

EXTENSION PUT IN
AFTER 1908

FISH
WHARF

MARINE PARADE SOUTH

EXTENSION PUT IN
AFTER 1908

(NOW SOUTH BEACH PARADE)

THE DRIVE
(SOUTH BEACH ROAD)

HARBOUR
MOUTH

GORLESTON
QUAY

BRUSH QUAY

BEACH

CHURCH
STREET

PIER
PLAIN

PIER
WALK

N

CAISTER ROAD DEPOT

OFFICES   ARMATURES

STORES

TURNTABLES

STABLES

MOULDINGS

BLACKSMITH

BODY SHOP
FITTERS SHOP

GORLESTON
DEPOT

HIGH STREET

BAKER STREET

To
GORLESTON
QUAY

LEGEND

TRAMWAYS CONSTRUCTED.
TRAMWAYS PROPOSED.
FORMER HORSE TRAMWAY.
OTHER ROADS.
RAILWAYS.

D.W.W. After R.C.A.   EA-4. 6-66

GREAT YARMOUTH
CORPORATION TRAMWAYS

0   ¼   ½   ¾   1

SCALE OF ONE MILE

GREAT YARMOUTH
ROAD

RIVER BURE

CAISTER

LAWN AVENUE

NORTHGATE
STREET

NORTH DRIVE

Specimen horse-car tickets.

Courtesy: C. Carter

British Thomson-Houston Company Limited, who both formed companies to work tramways in Great Yarmouth) were considered by the Corporation to be inadequate, and accordingly it was decided by 19 votes to 18 to carry on with the original proposal of municipal operation of the tramways. As a result of this further change in policy, Alderman Arnold resumed the chairmanship of the Tramways Committee.

By this time—1901—the price of steel rails had fallen to £5 18s. 6d. per ton, and accordingly 1,000 tons of steel girder rails were ordered from a Belgian firm; their quotation, including freightage, was less than any quotation received from a British firm.

Construction of the tramways was commenced on 16th October, 1901, and the rails were laid to a gauge of 3 ft. 6 in. The conventional overhead trolley line system was used. An examination of the map will clearly indicate the scheme; in brief it consisted of a tramway from a point near the depôt on Caister Road via Northgate Street, Market Place, King Street, Regent Road, and Marine Parade to Wellington Pier; a branch via Fullers' Hill to Vauxhall railway station, returning to King Street via the quays and Regent Street; an alternative route to Marine Parade via King Street and St. Peter's Road which had a triangular track layout at its junction with Marine Parade. A loop line was laid from Regent Road across Theatre Plain connecting the tramway in the Market Place with the Regent Road tramway. It all amounted to 1.90 miles of double line and 1.82 miles of single line. The maximum gradient was 1 in 27, and the minimum radius 48 ft.

Special trackwork being laid at the junction of St. Peter's Road and Marine Parade, Great Yarmouth.

The rails, which weighed 90 lb. per yard and were 7 in. deep with a groove of 1⅛ in., were laid on a bed of concrete made of sand and shingle from the beach and 1,500 tons of Portland cement; the road bed was paved with granite setts, lava basalt, asphalt cubes and Australian Jarrah wood blocks. Over half a million of these last were contracted for at a price that worked out at between 2d. and 3d. per block.

The British Insulated Wire Company of Prescot, Lancashire, supplied the poles and overhead equipment at a cost of £6,000. The overhead line was mainly supported by poles with bracket arms; the poles were painted brownish grey and had a considerable amount of ornamental scroll work. In Church Plain and the Market Place area, poles with span wires were used, while on the quays and Marine Parade, centre poles were used—these again had a good share of ornamental scrollwork. Feeder cables were supplied by the Telegraph Manufacturing Co. for £3,000; Messrs. Askham Bros. and Wilson of Sheffield supplied the special track work for the points and crossings, and the Brush Electrical Engineering Company of Loughborough supplied the first 14 cars at a cost of £7,843.

At the Corporation electricity works, structural alterations were necessary to accommodate the additional plant required by reason of the introduction of the tramways. These alterations were carried out to the directions of Mr. Eastoe; new generating machinery with a capacity of 400 kilowatts was installed, together with two new boilers.

Messrs. Crompton (now Crompton-Parkinson Ltd.) of Chelmsford supplied the storage battery and booster.

The depôt and offices at Caister Road were built by Messrs. Grimble and Harman. Accommodation was provided for 20 cars on four tracks and the interior of the building was lined with white and green enamelled bricks. Carting, paving, making up of roads, street improvements and the like made up the total cost of around £50,000.

An interesting feature of the Caister Road depôt was the three turntables leading to the three tracks into the body shop and fitters shop.

Also proposed at the time, but in the event not constructed, were a loop tramway via South Quay and Friar's Lane to St. Peter's Road and an extension tramway via the Drive to the Harbour's Mouth.

As construction of the tramway neared completion, a meeting of the 18 members of the Tramways Committee, under the chairmanship of Alderman Arnold, was held on 9th May, 1902, to consider the scheme for working the services on the tramway. The then recently-appointed manager, F. L. Turner, was in attendance. It was proposed that two services should be operated, one from Wellington Pier to Caister Road via St. Peter's Road, King Street, and Northgate Street, and the other from Wellington Pier via Regent Road and Regent Street to Vauxhall railway station. Fares were to be arranged on a basis of approximately 1d. per mile, with a fare stage of 1d. to either of the four termini or intermediate points from King Street/Market Place, and a through fare of 2d. from Vauxhall railway station or Caister Road termini to Wellington Pier.

The Board of Trade inspection was made on the morning and afternoon of 19th June, 1902. Colonel von Donop inspected the cars and permanent way, and the inspectors travelled over the tramway in one of the new cars, accompanied by Major Cardew of Messrs. Preece and Cardew (the Corporation's consulting engineers), Alderman Arnold and the borough surveyor. The inspectors passed the tramway as fit for public service and on the same afternoon it was officially opened. For the opening, three cars dressed with flags toured the system, starting from the Caister Road terminus and travelling to Wellington Pier Gardens from where the procession returned to the Town Hall, after which the cars commenced general service for the public. In the procession, the first car had the top deck occupied by the band of the Prince of Wales' Own Norfolk Artillery, the second conveyed the Mayor and members of the Corporation, and the third carried more members of the Corporation and various officials. A contemporary account records that "in the interior of the cars rode several ladies."

At a speech made at the opening ceremony, it was stated that the system had been constructed in eight months, and at certain times work had proceeded both day and night. Other interesting points were that £5,000 had been paid in wages, and this was good for the town as the workpeople depended to a great extent on seasonal work; the work had been done under the general supervision of the borough surveyor ; and the Brush Electrical Engineering Company of Loughborough had delivered the fourteen cars within twelve weeks of receiving the order. A reference was also made to the experimental nature of the fares, which were to be reviewed but which in the light of events remained substantially unchanged until after the First World War. A further point mentioned was that it was proposed to acquire, electrify, and connect the Gorleston horse tramways to the main system.

Full public service commenced on Friday, 20th June, 1902.

During the first week of operation there were two instances of trolley arms breaking and the trolley heads falling to the ground. In the first incident, two visitors to Great Yarmouth sustained cuts and bruises but no serious injuries.

Great Yarmouth cars in original livery at Wellington Pier. Note the destination indicator boards below the headlamps.

41

For the first two weeks of operation receipts were £369 15s. 10d. with 72,540 passengers carried. For the first full annual statement of accounts for the year ended 31st March, 1903, the total revenue was £6,398 ; passengers carried were 1,306,148—this was for nine months.

When first introduced, both services operated alternately via Regent Road and St. Peter's Road, cars proceeding via Regent Road, turning into Theatre Plain, Market Place, and via Northgate Street to Caister Road or via Fuller's Hill (where a 3 m.p.h. speed limit was imposed because of the narrowness of the thoroughfare) to Vauxhall station. In the inward direction, cars proceeded from Vauxhall station via North Quay to King Street and thence via St. Peter's Road ; cars from Caister Road proceeded via Northgate Street, King Street and St. Peter's Road. It followed that to work alternately over the various routes, Regent Road should be substituted for St. Peter's Road.

This "one-way" working was not universally popular and was later abandoned, as on the "one-way" system, passengers would be set down at the bottom of Fuller's Hill with a walk back to the Haven Bridge, rather than being set down at a point conveniently near to the bridge as was the case when cars returned via North Quay and Hall Quay to Vauxhall railway station.

When the tramways opened, a far-sighted innovation was the fitting of telephones to various overhead line poles to enable staff to telephone to the depôt in the event of their requiring assistance or advice. Stopping places were indicated by metal signs, request stops with white lettering on a blue background and fare stages with white lettering on a red background. At the time of writing (1964) one such sign still exists on the west side of Caister Road, opposite the race course.

Wages in June, 1903, were: motormen 22s. per week and conductors 20s. In this month, the town council granted the staff an increase of 2s. The staff then wore a stripe which was liable to forfeiture in the event of misconduct, which also meant that the man concerned lost his additional 2s.

Horse buses were operating in Yarmouth at the time of the opening of the tramways, and the owners rather felt the pinch. To stimulate business they advertised "1d. all the way" in competition with the tramway's 2d. from terminus to terminus. However, the horse bus operators could not halt progress ; their "price war" was to no avail and only resulted in a gradual cessation of horse bus services. A number of wagonettes were, however, used on pleasure trips in connection with the holiday trade, and some survived until 1939.

During 1904, the Corporation received powers authorising them to construct a subway under the River Yare, or alternatively to span the river by means of a transporter bridge. In addition, they were authorised to widen the Haven Bridge approach and to carry out other street widenings and improvements.

In the same year, the Tramways Committee recommended to the town council a proposal, which was adopted, that certain nurses who had to travel about the town in the pursuit of their duties should be granted an annual pass valued at £3.

At this time tickets purchased in bulk by the Corporation cost 1d. per thousand, the Corporation retaining the right to advertise on the backs of the tickets.

It is interesting to examine the revenue account of the Great Yarmouth Corporation Tramways for the year ending 31st March, 1905, for it gives an interesting insight into the relative distribution of revenue.

Revenue account

	Average per car-mile (d.)	£	s.	d.	£	s.	d.
Traffic expenses							
Wages and uniforms, motormen and conductors	2.064	2,012	0	6			
Wages of other traffic employees	0.018	17	13	4			
Cleaning and oiling cars	0.270	263	7	8			
Cleaning, salting and sanding track	0.104	101	14	5			
Ticket check	0.212	206	7	7			
Miscellaneous	0.042	41	8	0			
	2.710				2,642	11	6
General expenses							
Salaries of general officers and staff	0.342	333	11	5			
Rents	0.021	20	0	0			
Rates and taxes	0.284	277	12	1			
Printing, stationery and advertising	0.036	35	3	8			
Fuel and water	0.030	28	16	1			
Accident insurances and compensations	0.122	119	2	5			
Fire and other insurances	0.014	14	5	0			
Miscellaneous	0.036	35	4	3			
	0.885				863	14	11

43

	Average per car-mile (d.)	£	s.	d.	£	s.	d.
General repairs and maintenance							
Permanent way	0.300	292	16	5			
Electrical equipment	0.140	135	17	4			
Buildings and fixtures	0.016	15	6	0			
Workshop tools and sundry plant	0.030	29	9	9			
Cars	0.489	476	12	6			
	0.975				950	2	0
Power expenses							
Electricity works for current	1.940				1,891	18	1
Total amount of working expenses	6.510				6,348	6	6
Balance carried to net revenue account					2,388	1	9
Traffic revenue	8.776	8,559	7	4			
Advertisements	0.181	177	0	11			
	8.957	8,736	8	3	8,736	8	3

Passengers carried — 3,642,400
Car miles run   —   468,130

On 14th October, 1904, the tramway was extended from St. Peter's Road, opposite the church, to Queen's Road via Blackfriar's Road, but the next major development was when the Gorleston horse tramway was electrified. The Corporation negotiated the purchase of the horse tramway company as a going concern, and completed the purchase in March, 1905, when the business was bought for £13,211 11s. 3d., the amount being exclusive of the shares in the steamboat company and of certain stores and buses.

During 1904—the last full year of operation on the horse tramway—1,193,338 passengers were conveyed and receipts amounted to £6,964. This may be compared with the figures for the first year of operation by the B.E.T.—1900—which were 965,238 and £6,369 respectively.

The work of electrification was commenced immediately by the Corporation under the supervision of the borough surveyor, and gave employment to between 500 and 600 men. It cost £52,000 for the purchase and electrification of the horse tramway, so in round figures the Corporation tramways had cost about £120,000—including extensions. At Gorleston, Feather's Plain, a new depôt was erected in ten weeks on a site adjacent to the old horse car depôt.

During the work, horse buses from the replaced Yarmouth services bridged the gap between the Haven Bridge and the point where the tramway was being relaid. The last horse car was driven by a driver named Carter who had driven the first car over the tramway 30 years previously.

The electrified tramway was opened for traffic on 4th July, 1905, with the official opening ceremony performed by the Mayor, who drove the first of three decorated cars from Southtown to Gorleston. Alderman Arnold drove the second car, and the party consisted of members of the Corporation, the Tramways Committee, and other invited guests and officials. On the inaugural journey the party inspected the depôt before proceeding to the terminus near Gorleston Beach where they alighted and proceeded to the Cliff Hotel for a civic luncheon.

The Gorleston section ran almost as a separate undertaking. The staff there consisted of the cashier, a clerk, two inspectors and a relief, a foreman, four night cleaners, one day cleaner, a body-builder, and three car mechanics. All major work was done at Gorleston up to and including painting, but the painter was sent out from Caister Road. The heavy mechanical work was done at Caister Road and the components were sent to Gorleston depôt for assembly into the car concerned.

Opening of the electrified tramway from the Haven Bridge to Gorleston on 4th July, 1905. These cars were of the second batch and the revised location of the destination indicator should be noted.

45

An early view of No. 19 at Feathers Plain, Gorleston.

The tramway from Southtown to Gorleston divided at Gorleston, Feather's Plain (the stage now known as Gorleston Library), then one tramway was routed to the beach and the other along the main Lowestoft Road to Gorleston railway station. It was at the last-named point that the East Anglian Light Railway Company Limited had proposed to commence their tramway from Gorleston to Lowestoft and Kessingland. (See Lowestoft Corporation Tramways, chapter 5.)

Returning to the inaugural journey over the electrified horse tramway and the civic luncheon, it is worth noting that at the speechmaking it was said that "it would be utterly impossible to make it thoroughly successful unless they (the Corporation) took the tram lines over the bridge." But although this was often considered (in fact a decision to widen the bridge was taken by the Corporation on 14th September, 1905), nothing ever came of it and the two parts of the undertaking remained divided.

In 1905, twelve new cars were purchased (Nos. 15–26) and ten of them were allocated to the Southtown–Gorleston tramway.

The story of the horse tramway is not quite complete without the details of the sale held at Yareside Stables, Southtown, by direction of Yarmouth Corporation. The sale was attended by a large number of prospective buyers who came from all parts of the eastern counties between London and York and there was much brisk bidding. Arthur B. Castle was the auctioneer, and before the sale he made a rather nostalgic speech, saying that although the horses had worked hard, especially during the period of electrification of the tramway when considerable obstructions were placed in their way as a result of the road works, they were all good horses. The items for sale consisted of the stud of 60 horses, the trams and buses, the remainder of the car harnesses, and all the stable equipment. The prices which the better known horses fetched were:

Bay mare	Baby	15 hands 3 in.	35 gn.
Bay mare	Stone	16 hands 1 in.	17 gn.
Bay mare	Starchy	15 hands 3 in.	21 gn.
Bay horse	Prince	16 hands 2½ in.	20 gn.
Bay mare	Tiny	15 hands 2 in.	22 gn.
Bay horse	Tom	16 hands	27 gn.
Black horse	Cockrell	16 hands	17 gn.
Bay mare	Filly	16 hands 2 in.	27 gn.
Chestnut horse	Ping Pong	16 hands	23 gn.
Bay mare	Caister	16 hands	21 gn.
Brown horse	Trilby	15 hands 2½ in.	20 gn.
Roan mare	Roany	16 hands	26 gn.
Brown horse	Palmer	16 hands	29 gn.
Bay horse	Jimmy	16 hands	20 gn.
Bay mare	Polly	15 hands 2¼ in.	17 gn.
Bay mare	Lopsy Popsy	16 hands 1 in.	30 gn.
Brown mare	Bonnie	16 hands 1 in.	19 gn.
Bay horse	Smasher	16 hands 1 in.	16½ gn.
Black horse	Samson	16 hands	17 gn.
Black mare	Bess	15 hands 2¼ in.	27 gn.

Five trams, each capable of carrying 46 passengers, with lamps, poles and bars, were sold for 8 gn. to 10½ gn. each. The Race Committee of the Corporation purchased one, the Fish Wharf Committee one, a person at Belton secured another, and the other two were sold to residents at Wroxham and Leiston. It must be presumed that the other cars were sold prior to the auction.

Immediately the Gorleston line was electrified, work commenced on the extension to the Fish Wharf, and during the first week of July (1905) possession was taken of Barrack Street, the road torn up, the concrete bed formed and the track laying commenced. Work proceeded rapidly and on Sunday, 8th August, 1905, the extension was opened to traffic. The final major extension was opened on 16th May, 1907, when the Caister Road tramway was extended outside the borough boundary to Caister; five new cars (Nos. 27–31) were acquired to work this service. A short extension was laid further into Admiralty Road from its junction with Barrack Road some time between 1908 and 1910, although the service to the Fish Wharf normally operated via Barrack Road.

This completed the development of the tramways; the mileage constructed was 9.94 miles, while 0.06 miles was authorised but not constructed. Of the constructed mileage, 4.80 miles were double track and 5.13 miles single track. The last cars to be purchased were Nos. 32–35, and they were delivered to the Corporation in 1907 at a cost of £520 each. Of the rolling stock, fifteen cars were allocated to Gorleston depôt and the remainder to Caister Road depôt.

Services and fares

At this time the services operated and relative fares were as follows:

SOUTHTOWN (foot of Haven Bridge)—GORLESTON PIER (Winter)/GORLESTON BEACH (Summer) or GORLESTON RAILWAY STATION

Service operated every 15 minutes during the winter, alternate cars operating to Gorleston (beach) or Gorleston (railway station). In the summer (July and August) the service operated every 7½ minutes with the same alternate working except that "Beach" cars were extended to Gorleston (Pavilion).

> *Single Fares*
> Haven Bridge
> 1d. Halfway House
> 2d. 1d. Gorleston Termini

WELLINGTON PIER—MARKET PLACE—NORTHGATE ST.—CAISTER-ON-SEA

Service operated every 15 minutes.

> *Single Fares*
> Wellington Pier
> 1d. Top of Regent Road or Theatre Plain
> 2d. 1d. Newtown
> 3d. 2d. 1d. Caister

WELLINGTON PIER—REGENT ST.—VAUXHALL RAILWAY STATION

Service operated every 10 minutes, and for some years before its abandonment was only operated during the summer months.

> *Single Fares*
> Wellington Pier
> 1d. Top of Regent Road
> 2d. 1d. Vauxhall Rly. Station

NEWTOWN (CAISTER ROAD)—KING ST.—FISH WHARF
(With occasional short workings to Fuller's Hill)
Service operated every 10 minutes during the winter with extra cars during the summer period and in the herring season.

Single Fares
Newtown
1d. Top of Regent Road
2d. 1d. Fish Wharf

These service frequencies remained much the same throughout the life of the tramways, but the fares changed. An interesting feature was the issue of "discount" tickets at 1s. 3d. per dozen.

Colour light signals were installed on the following sections of the tramway:

Hall Quay to top of Regent Road
Halfway House to Barking Fishery
Baker Street to Pier Walk
Pier Walk to Gorleston Quay

"Next Car" clocks were installed at Caister, Gorleston Quay, and Southtown railway station. Waiting shelters were installed at Caister terminus, Newtown (Beaconsfield Road), Vauxhall station, Wellington Pier, Fish Wharf, Southtown Bridge, Halfway House, Gorleston depôt, Gorleston Quay, and Gorleston railway station.

The average speed of the services considered as a group was 7.41 miles per hour.

1914–1920
As with most tramway undertakings, the Yarmouth system came out of the First World War in a bad state, having lacked much maintenance due to shortage of parts, raw materials, and—equally important—skilled craftsmen who had been conscripted into the armed forces. Consequently, at the cessation of hostilities, much money had to be spent on repairs and renewals, but this was mainly spent on the track and the betterment of rolling stock as no new cars were purchased—the impact of the internal combustion engine had not been really felt in 1920, but it was not far off.

At a meeting of the Tramways Committee in June, 1920, a special sub-committee was formed to consider the operation of buses. In September, 1920, the committee authorised the tramways manager to purchase three such vehicles. As a result, the Corporation obtained three second-hand, open-top double-deck "B" type buses from the

49

D

London General Omnibus Co. Ltd. at a cost of £1,725. These vehicles retained their L.G.O.C. red and white livery throughout their career, but had the Corporation's coat-of-arms on the waist panel in place of "General." The top deck sides carried full-length advertisements with the words "Travel by Tram." On 6th October, 1920, these vehicles commenced operating a service between Cobholm, High Mill Road, and Britannia Pier, to augment the existing tramway service between Vauxhall railway station, Town Hall and Wellington Pier. Fares were: Cobholm and Theatre Plain 1½d.; Cobholm and Britannia Pier 2d.

1920–1933

A general fares revision in 1922 resulted in all single fares being increased by 50 per cent as follows:

Haven Bridge
1½d. Halfway House
3d. 1½d. Gorleston Termini

Wellington Pier
1½d. Top of Regent Road
3d. 1½d. Vauxhall Rly. Station

Wellington Pier
1½d. Top of Regent Rd. or Theatre Plain
3d. 1½d. Newtown
4½d. 3d. 2d. Caister

Newtown
1½d. Top of Regent Road
3d. 1½d. Fish Wharf

The original manager, F. L. Turner, resigned in May, 1922, and P. G. Campling was appointed in his place.

No. 29, a car of the third batch, about to turn from the Marine Parade into Regent Road, Great Yarmouth.

No. 34, a car of the final batch, at Wellington Pier in 1932 working on the through service to Caister-on-Sea. The opening window frames are clearly distinguishable. *Photo: M. J. O'Connor*

The buses were a success, and as a result of the experiment, the Tramways Committee decided to obtain powers to abandon the tramway from King Street to the Fish Wharf, replacing the tramway service with a bus service. The necessary powers were obtained, and in 1924 seven single-deck buses (Nos. 1–7) were acquired. They replaced the Newtown–Fish Wharf tramway service on 15th May, 1924, operation of that tramway having ceased on 14th May. At the same time as this service ceased, the tramways in St. Peter's Road and from near Vauxhall station via Fuller's Hill to Church Plain were abandoned. The rails, however, remained in Fuller's Hill to the end of tramway operation, although elsewhere the rails were lifted soon after the services ceased over the roads concerned.

Between 1924 and 1926 nearly all the track of the remaining tramways was renewed and this put a crippling debt on the undertaking which was not eliminated until towards the end of the 1939–45 war. One of the aspects of the track renewal was that, as a result of the extra cars which had to operate via Theatre Plain, due to the abandonment of the St. Peter's Road tramway, the single-line section in the Market Place was doubled and the loop at the seaward end of Regent Road was extended.

During the years to 1928, nine more motor buses (Nos. 8–16) were purchased and used to introduce a new service between Yarmouth (Regal Theatre) and Gorleston (Elmhurst) or Gorleston Links (Links Lane); alternate buses operated to Gorleston Links at intervals of 30 minutes, thereby providing a 15-minute service between Yarmouth and Gorleston (Elmhurst). The service to Gorleston Links operated between Halfway House and Gorleston Library via Beccles Road, Church Road, and Church Lane. Also started in 1928 was an early morning journey from Gorleston depôt to Vauxhall station to connect with a train for Norwich; a return facility was provided in the evening in the opposite direction.

A service cut had taken place in 1929 when the Wellington Pier to Caister-on-Sea tramway service was truncated at the Market Place, but later in the year the service resumed operating through to Wellington Pier in the evenings after 6.30 p.m. The cars terminated on the spur in King Street at the top of Regent Road when on the short working to the Market Place. The tramway service from the Wellington Pier to Vauxhall railway station ceased on Sunday, 6th October, 1929, and new buses Nos. 17–21 were used to replace the trams.

At the end of the 1930 summer season, the Tramways Manager estimated that £30,000 would have to be spent to renew and repair the track and cars of the two remaining tramways, i.e. Southtown to

No. 6 in the Market Place, Great Yarmouth. It will be observed that the track had been doubled when this photograph was taken but this car still retained reversed staircases and high front destination indicators.

Guy 'FCX' double-deck bus, one of a batch used to replace the cars on the tramway to Gorleston. *Photo: Great Yarmouth Corporation*

Gorleston, and Wellington Pier to Caister-on-Sea. As a result of this and the fact that the buses had proved so successful, the Corporation decided to secure powers to abandon the remaining two tramways and substitute buses.

To strengthen the position of the bus service between Yarmouth and Gorleston, and at the same time to meet public requests, the tramway from Southtown to Gorleston was abandoned on 25th September, 1930, and a through bus service from Yarmouth (Market Place) to Gorleston (Beach) and Gorleston (Cliffs) was introduced ; this was operated by double- and single-deck vehicles, five more of which were purchased during 1930 (Nos. 22–26). The same year saw a change of management when H. A. Blackburn succeeded P. G. Campling as manager.

On the occasion of the Municipal Passenger Transport Association Conference held in Yarmouth in 1931, a Garrett single-deck trolleybus was operated from Yarmouth to Caister, using one trolley on the overhead line and a skate running in the tramway rail. At this time it is believed that Yarmouth Corporation considered the introduction of trolleybuses, but no development of this proposal was proceeded with.

The year 1931 saw the next purchase of double-deck vehicles when five A.E.C. Regents (Nos. 27–31) were obtained.

53

The ticket system in use was the "Bell Punch" system, using preprinted card tickets and a numerically registering punch. Tickets in use on the tramway and bus services were as follows:

Value	Colour	Value	Colour
1d.	Yellow	8d. Return	Salmon
1½d.	Brown	9d. Return	Dark brown
2d.	Green	10d. Return	Dark grey
2½d.	Pink	Workpeople's ticket	Yellow
3d.	White	Workpeople's exchange ticket	Yellow
3½d.	Purple	Employee's exchange ticket	White with diagonal red cross
4d.	White with blue overprint on stage numbers	2d. parcel ticket	Green
		3d. parcel ticket	Salmon
4½d.	Blue	2d. dog ticket	Red
5d.	Pale green	Free blind person's ticket	Dark brown
6d.	Orange	Discount ticket	Light grey

The "Bell Punch" parcel tickets actually had sticky backs. Any article which was carried on the front of the car under the staircase was charged 2d. Unaccompanied parcels were charged 3d.

The last tramway service to survive was the one from Wellington Pier to Caister-on-Sea and this continued until 1933, when the last car was operated with some ceremony. This car, No. 6, which was lettered "Progress" on the front and "1902. Tramways. 1933," and "1933. Motor Buses?" on the sides, was brilliantly illuminated; 320 coloured electric lamps were used to form a decorative pattern. The car had

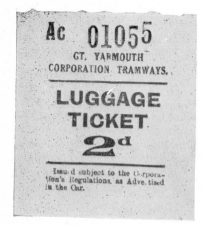

A selection of Great Yarmouth Corporation tickets.

No. 3 at the Caister terminus. Note the rebuilt staircases and the destination indicator under the canopy. A view taken in latter days.

Photo: M. J. O'Connor

No. 15 in final style at Wellington Pier, Great Yarmouth, in 1932.

Photo: M. J. O'Connor

operated on several occasions during the summer and autumn of 1933 between Caister and Yarmouth while the sea front was illuminated. On No. 6's final journey from the Market Place to the depôt on Friday, 14th December, 1933, the car was crewed by members of the Council, the Mayor, Peter Ellis, driving, and Alderman Arthur Beevor conducting. Other members of the Council were the passengers. The car was crowded—including a number of standing passengers—and on the platform with the Mayor were H. A. Blackburn, the Transport Manager, and the Traffic Superintendent, H. G. Styles.

A large crowd had assembled at the Market Place to see the car leave on the final journey, and as it travelled non-stop to the depôt, fog detonators exploded on the track. In his capacity as conductor, Alderman Beevor—twice Mayor of Yarmouth and, incidentally, a one-time conductor on the old horse tramway—collected £2 4s. 2d. which was sent to the Mayor's Christmas Parcel Fund.

At the depôt, the party on the last car was entertained to tea in the mess room at the invitation of E. V. Barr, Chairman of the Transport Committee, and afterwards the party visited the garage and offices. At the closing, Barr made a speech in the course of which he said that had Shakespeare been the conductor on the last car he might have said:

"Farewell, old tram, no more can you be mended ;
    Go rest in peace
Your useful life has ended."

The replacement bus service was identical with the service which had been operated on the tramways, i.e. every 15 minutes during the day to the town centre, the service being extended to the Wellington Pier in the evenings during the winter and all day during the summer.

Twenty-five of the cars ended their days as chalets at Caister Holiday Camp, and the bodies of the two last cars to run in Gorleston and Yarmouth respectively were finished in aluminium paint and stood on the marsh between Yarmouth and Caister on a site adjoining the greyhound racing stadium.

Although most of the rails have been lifted, the tramway in Caister Road has been left *in situ* as reinforcement for the carriageway which is rather unstable. The track fans still exist in the depôt at Caister Road, although the depôt and offices have been much rebuilt and extended to house the municipal fleet of buses.

A side view of the 'standard' Great Yarmouth car.

At Gorleston, at a point in Lowestoft Road just south of its junction with Bakers Road, there is a public house called "The Tramway Hotel." The signboard has a painting of a Yarmouth Corporation car.

Schedule of cars

The 35 cars owned by the Corporation tramways were supplied by the Brush Electrical Engineering Co. of Loughborough and they followed the standard pattern of the time in having Brush-built four-window open-top double-deck bodies mounted on Brush four-wheel trucks each with two Brush 25 h.p. motors.

1–14

Built and delivered for the opening of the tramways in 1902, these cars as built had reversed staircases, canopies over the platforms, and seated 56 persons, 34 outside and 22 inside. The lower deck was panelled in polished wood, and had longitudinal wooden seats, while outside there were wooden "lift over" garden seats. Besides hand brakes, the cars also had rheostatic brakes. The trolleys were of the swivel-head type.

Originally the destination of the car was displayed by means of a board hung on the dash below the headlamp, but at a later date a roller blind destination indicator was mounted on top of the upper deck rails at each end of the car. Another modification came about when the destination indicator box was hung from the underside of the canopy over the platform. The cars carried the following place names on their destination blinds (it should be noted that they were, for obvious reasons, split into those operating in Gorleston and those in Yarmouth proper):

Caister Road depôt cars	*Gorleston depôt cars*
WELLINGTON PIER	HAVEN BRIDGE
NEWTOWN	GORLESTON STATION
CAISTER-ON-SEA	GORLESTON BEACH
TOP OF REGENT ROAD	GORLESTON QUAY
FISH WHARF	GORLESTON DEPOT
VAUXHALL STATION	HALFWAY HOUSE
MARKET PLACE	SPECIAL
RACE COURSE	
SPECIAL	

A further modification was the substitution of half-turn staircases for the reversed staircases, thereby reducing the outside seating to 32 seats. It is interesting to note that No. 6 retained its reversed staircases and top-deck destination indicator until as late as 1925. No. 6 was the 'last car,' and perhaps points to the supposition that it was the final car to be rebuilt.

15–26

Ten of these cars were used on the Southtown–Gorleston tramway and were, in fact, delivered for the opening of this tramway as an electrified line. Built in 1905, they were similar to the first batch except that they had half-turn staircases and destination indicators on the top deck rails when delivered. An additional feature was four air scoop ventilators each side of the car. At a later date the destination indicator was removed from the top deck position and fitted under the canopy.

27–31

These cars followed the pattern of 15–26 and were built for the opening of the Caister extension tramway.

32–35

On these cars, which were built to the pattern of the previous cars, the windows could be independently lowered.

Livery

Dashes, stair stringers, upper side panels and lower deck ventilation boards: maroon; rocker panels, window frames, underside of stairs and top deck decency screens: cream. The Corporation's coat-of-arms was displayed midway on the upper (maroon) side panels and the title "GT. YARMOUTH CORPORATION TRAMWAYS" on the rocker panel (cream). The car's number was displayed on the dash above the headlight. Maroon panels were lined out in gold, and cream panels lined out in black.

Car allocation

Twenty cars were allocated to Caister Road depôt and fifteen to Gorleston depôt.

A Great Yarmouth Corporation car decorated in true nautical style.

CHAPTER FOUR

IPSWICH

Pre-1900

THE history of Ipswich is readily traced back to the time of the battle of Hastings, 1066, but it is to the nineteenth century that one must look to see the beginning of the development of modern Ipswich. In 1809 a new provision and cattle market was built ; in 1812 a new corn exchange ; in 1818 the foundation stone was laid for a new town hall ; and in 1817 an "East Indiaman," the Orwell, of 1,400 tons, was launched. The population was increasing and in 1837 the first Ipswich Dock Act was passed, but it was the coming of the railway which put the town on its feet. Further Dock Acts were passed in 1852, 1877, 1881 and 1898, empowering the River Commissioners to build docks and construct locks.

Following the development of the port, there was progress in the field of industry, and factories were established for the manufacture of agricultural implements, fertilisers and clothing, and for shipbuilding, mechanical engineering, flour milling and allied industries. The docks were further developed, and to meet all these new ventures, cheap transport was necessary to convey the employees from their homes to the industrial sites, which were located in the region of the docks and along the banks of the River Orwell. The housing development was mainly carried out first to the north-west of the town and then to the east and south-east of the town, giving a logical movement of traffic for a public transport system.

In a similar manner to the introduction of street tramways into other cities and towns in Britain, tramways were introduced into Ipswich towards the end of the nineteenth century. The first moves came in 1879 when Simon Armstrong Graham of Manchester obtained a Provisional Order permitting him to construct and work a system of horse tramways in Ipswich, and as a result a 3 ft. 6 in. gauge horse tramway of about three-quarter route miles was opened on 10th October, 1880, between Cornhill and the railway station.

A further Order was obtained in 1880, and then in 1881 the Ipswich Tramways Act was passed, incorporating the Ipswich Tramway Com-

61

pany, with James Robertson as trustee, and William Bruce Dick—of the firm Dick, Kerr and Co.—and Peter Bruff as principal directors, to take over the two previous Orders. The newly-formed company then proceeded under the same Act to make a number of extensions to the existing system. The first addition was from Princes Street/ Portman Road junction to Barrack Road corner via Portman Road and Mill Street, and the second was an extension from the Cornhill via Westgate Street, St. Matthew's Street, Barrack Corner, and Norwich Road to Brook's Hall (Norwich Road). In 1884 the final extension of the horse tramway system took place when a tramway was opened from the Cornhill via Major's Corner and St. John's Road to Derby Road railway station; this completed the cross-town link and gave a maximum route mileage of 4.4 miles. During the late 1880s, the tramway in Portman Road and Mill Street was abandoned.

Rolling stock consisted of a mixed fleet of single-and double-deck four-wheel cars. It is believed that the cars were built by the Starbuck Car and Wagon Company. They were delivered in three batches as follows:

Nos. 1–3. Single-deck, entered service 10th October, 1880.
Nos. 4–6. Double-deck, entered service 1882. Garden seats.
Nos. 7–9. Double-deck, entered service 1884. Garden seats.

Livery was maroon and cream, with the fleet name "Ipswich Tramway Company" on the rocker panels.

Motive power was provided by a stud of 27 horses; single-deck cars had one horse and double-deck cars two horses. Horse bus services were also in operation in Ipswich, worked by double-deck buses each with two horses; trace horses assisted in pulling the buses up St. John's Hill.

During 1899, the Ipswich Town Council decided to proceed with a scheme for acquiring the horse tramway system and converting it to electric traction, at the same time making a number of extensions to other parts of the borough not served by the horse tramways. Accordingly, the Parliamentary Committee of the Corporation negotiated the purchase and in 1899 opened negotiations with the Ipswich Tramways Company. Unfortunately, the company could not accept the Corporation's terms of purchase and the Corporation gave notice to purchase under their Tramways Act which they had obtained in 1900.

1900–1914

In February, 1901, the Ipswich Tramways Company wrote to the Board of Trade asking them to nominate an arbitrator to determine the amount to be paid by the Corporation for their undertaking. The

Double-deck horse-drawn car of the Ipswich Tramways Company.

Horse-drawn cars, both single-deck and double-deck, can be seen in this view of the Cornhill, Ipswich. *Photo: Courtesy J. H. Price*

Board of Trade appointed Sir Frederick Bramwell to act as arbitrator. After hearing a considerable amount of evidence at various hearings, he gave his award, that the price to be paid by the Corporation for the company was £17,552. The capital expenditure of the company was £33,139, according to their balance sheets.

The Ipswich Corporation Tramways Act of 1900 authorised them to work tramways, to construct additional tramways, and to introduce electric lighting into the borough. Messrs. Kennedy and Jenkins of London were appointed engineers to the Corporation for the joint tramway and lighting scheme. Construction commenced in 1902, but some difficulty was experienced at the site of the power station and tramway depôt—Seven Acre Field—due to the swampy nature of the ground which was near the river, and a bed of concrete 40 ft. deep and 40 ft. square was necessary to support the stack.

The horse tramway system continued to be operated by the Corporation until such time as the permanent-way work for the electric tramway commenced, but the operation of the horse tramway only resulted in a financial loss for the Corporation. As a result, the services on the horse tramway were abandoned on 6th June, 1903, to permit the electrical equipment to be speedily installed. As far as can be ascertained, few changes took place under Corporation "rule" except that the company's name on the cars was replaced by the Corporation crest.

In September, 1903, Ipswich Corporation received the sanction of the Board of Trade to the borrowing of £61,164 for the following purposes and periods:

Permanent-way, land, buildings, etc.—30 years, £39,933.
Electrical equipment, with contingencies—20 years, £10,831.
Cars—£10,400.

Before considering the actual extensions made, it is worth considering, in general terms, the physical construction of the tramways. A gauge of 3 ft. 6 in. was chosen for a number of reasons, not least of which was the extreme narrowness of a number of the streets in which double-track tramway was laid—because to have laid a standard-gauge tramway with single track would have meant that no traffic could have passed on either side of a tramway car. In one instance, a street in which double-track tramway was laid was only 15 ft. 10 in. wide, and the rail nearest the kerb was, in places, laid with a gap of only 3 ft. between the outer rails and the kerbs of the footpath. The tramway was laid along one side of the roadway at the approaches to each side of Stoke Bridge.

Curves were numerous; seven were less than 50 ft. radius and at Major's Corner the radius was 40 ft. Fortunately, gradients were not severe; only three were steeper than 1 in 15, and the worst was 1 in 11½ for a distance of 45 yards up Bishop's Hill on the route to the Royal Oak.

The rails, which were grooved steel girder in 45-ft. lengths weighing 90 lb. per yard, were supplied by the North Eastern Steel Company. "Dicker" joints were used throughout, both for the ordinary track and for the special work and points, which were supplied by Hadfields Steel Foundry Company. The fishplates used were 2 ft. long, weighed 58 lb. per yard, and were secured with six bolts secured with split pins. Tie-bars, ⅞ in. thick, were spaced at 9 ft. intervals. For the track part of the circuit there were two solid crown bonds per joint, each bond of 0.166-square-inch section to a length of 2 ft. 5½ in. The cross bonds between the rails of the single track were 120 ft. apart and, in the case of the double track, the cross bonds between the tracks were at intervals of 240 ft.

The track was laid on a six-inch-thick bed of concrete with wood block paving in the centre of the town and stone blocks on the more suburban routes. The permanent-way construction was carried out by Dick, Kerr and Company Limited, but the Corporation had the paving work carried out as a separate contract from the laying of the permanent way. When completed the system amounted to 4.20 miles of double track and 6.62 miles of single track, making 10.82 route miles, for which the permanent way construction cost was £41,220.

The overhead trolley line, which was double throughout, using a trolley line of 0.325-inch diameter, was hung by means of bracket arms from tubular overhead poles spaced at intervals on an average of about 115 feet. The overhead trolley line was divided into half-mile sections and in all there were 22½ miles of trolley lines. The overhead poles were supplied by John Spencer Limited to the British Electric Equipment Company, which erected all the overhead line equipment; although this was mainly of the bracket arm type, span wire construction was used in places, particularly in the town centre. The seven feeder cables were made by Messrs. Johnson and Phillips Limited. An interesting feature was the installation of a telephone in each switch box for direct communication with the power station.

As mentioned earlier, a power station was built on Seven Acre Field which fronted on to Constantine Road, and the car shed was also built on this site—in fact it adjoined the power station. The power

65

station buildings were designed by C. Stanley Peach—a London architect—and erected by the firm of Sidney A. Kenney of Ipswich.

In the boiler house of the power station were four boilers of marine type, each suitable for a steam pressure of 160 lb. per square inch ; they were supplied by Danks of Oldbury. The four engines were by Reavell and Company Limited of Ipswich; the two larger were 360 i.h.p. running at 350 r.p.m., and the other two were 200 i.h.p. running at 450 r.p.m. (The Reavell engines had the feature that in principle each cylinder was a sort of combination of high and low pressure cylinder in that fresh steam was allowed to mix with the compressed steam on the exhaust stroke.) Each engine was shaft governed and coupled direct to its generator, which was an eight-pole unit supplied by A.E.G. of Berlin.Traction voltage was 500 volts d.c.

The switchboard, which was also supplied by A.E.G., was of white marble and had 23 panels, nine of which were for lighting and traction feeders. There were also panels for each dynamo and booster, two battery panels (for use in connection with the storage batteries), and one Board of Trade panel. Instruments were mostly by Elliott Brothers. The capacity of the power station was 8,720 kilowatts (about 11,700 h.p.).

An interior view of Ipswich depôt in 1904.

Adjoining the power station was the repair shop which was equipped with lifting jacks, wheel presses, and lathes, besides all the other necessary equipment and tools for the overhaul and maintenance of tramway cars. The entire width of the shop was spanned by a travelling crane, supplied by Ransomes and Rapier, Ipswich, which could lift ten tons. The car shed had eight tracks (with an access track leading off into the repair shop) and could accommodate 40 cars. The shed was divided into three bays 180 feet long by 87 feet wide. The whole area of the ground below the car shed had been excavated, and the flooring rested on piers ten feet apart, an arrangement which made for ease of maintenance and inspection of the underside of the cars. To complete the building, offices were added for use of the manager, other officials, clerks, and motormen and conductors, for whom there was also a mess-room.

It was a dull day, unfortunately, on Saturday, 21st November, 1903, when the Mayoress of Ipswich unlocked and opened the main doorway at the tramway offices with a silver key, by which simple ceremony the Ipswich Corporation Tramways were declared open. After this opening Mr. Jervis, the Chairman of the Ipswich Tramways and Lighting Committee, entertained the invited guests to a civic lunch in the specially decorated repair shop. During the course of his speech Jervis stated that £110,000 had been spent on the tramways and £43,000 on street widenings—work which had entirely altered the appearance of certain localities. At the conclusion of the lunch, the guests boarded special cars for a tour over the tramways.

Public services on the tramways commenced on Monday, 23rd November, 1903, but this day was also ill-fated because at 3.40 p.m. No. 20 was derailed at the top of Princes Street. The combined efforts of Nos. 8 and 24 were required to re-rail the derailed car. On the next day—Tuesday—the power supply failed, but after these teething troubles the Corporation's luck changed and such mishaps became rare. For the opening of the tramways, cars Nos. 1–26 had been delivered, and Nos. 27–36 followed shortly afterwards.

The final total cost of constructing and equipping the tramways and power station was as follows:

Tramways ...	£119,460 17s. 11d.	(or £ 9,460 17s. 11d. in excess of estimate)
Power station	£ 71,184 5s. 1d.	(or £ 7,637 0s. 1d. in excess of estimate)
Street widenings	£ 44,466 9s. 4d.	(or £ 1,466 9s. 4d. in excess of estimate)
Other items of minor character	£ 1,355 0s. 6d.	(or £ 355 0s. 6d. in excess of estimate)
Total cost ...	£236,466 12s. 10d.	(or £18,919 7s. 10d. in excess of estimate)

The Cornhill, Ipswich, focal point of the town's tramway system.
Photo: Courtesy W. E. Deamer

Another view of the Cornhill in Ipswich.

By far the greater part of the system was laid with single track and there were frequent passing loops; only in the main street from Barrack Corner in the west to Major's Corner in the east was double track predominant, and this extended for about a mile. At the central point—the Cornhill—there was a double-track tramway, and the track was also laid double around the "S" bend in Queen Street.

The Cornhill was the focal point of the system and it was from here that the routes radiated to the various parts of the borough. For that reason it is most convenient to describe each route separately and then consider the services which operated over them.

Cornhill–Whitton

Laid as a double track to Barrack Corner and thence single track with passing loops along Norwich Road, past Brook Hall, to High Street, Whitton. There was sufficient clearance under the railway bridge which crossed the Norwich Road to permit the passage of double-deck cars without difficulty or road works, but there was a notice painted on the bridge as follows: "Passengers are requested to keep their seats while the car is passing under the bridge." At one time cars showed "Norwich Road" as destination but this was later changed to "Whitton." This was the most northerly of the Ipswich Corporation's tramway routes and the Whitton–Brook's Hill section was originally a section of the horse tramway network.

No. 36, the highest-numbered car in the fleet, at the railway bridge in Norwich Road; the wording on the bridge reads: "Passengers are requested to keep their seats while the car is passing under the bridge."

Cornhill–Derby Road (railway station)

This tramway was laid with double track along Tavern Street and thence single track with passing loops along the old horse tramway route which was via Major's Corner, Spring Road, St. John's Road, Cauldwellhall Road, to Derby Road railway station. When electrification took place a spur was laid into the yard of the station, and though not regularly used this was a great asset when special excursion trains were operated from the station.

Cornhill–Royal Oak

Via Major's Corner, Upper Orwell Street, Fore Street, Fore Hamlet, Bishops Hill (the steepest gradient on the tramways was on this hill), Felixstowe Road, to the Royal Oak. Cars going to Royal Oak showed "Felixstowe Road" on the destination board.

Cornhill–Bourne Bridge

Via Queen Street, Bridge Street, Stoke Bridge, Vernon Street, Wherstead Road, to Bourne Bridge. Another bridge, carrying a standard-gauge dock tramway, crosses Wherstead Road, and when the tramway was laid it was necessary to lower the road a matter of two feet in order to achieve the required clearance of 16 ft. 4in. A further standard-gauge dock tramway crossed the electric tramway on the level just north of Stoke Bridge.

No. 28 passing the picturesque Wolsey Pharmacy.

Cars 10 and 14 at the Great Eastern Railway station; No. 14 appears to
have become dewired.   *Photo: Courtesy J. H. Price*

On the south side of Stoke Bridge a tramway was laid along Burrell
Road to the railway station, and still further south along Wherstead
Road a branch tramway was laid along Bath Street. Apparently the
reason was to provide a service between the railway station and the
Quay from which Great Eastern Railway paddle steamers sailed on
trips down the River Orwell to Felixstowe.

Cornhill–Railway Station
Via Princes Street and Station Drive to the railway station, this was
the route of the original horse tramway. The abandoned horse tramway between Barrack Corner and Princes Street via Mill Street and
Portman Road was resurrected for depôt access when the tramways
were electrified. This latter tramway was laid with single track and,
while not forming part of the route of any service, it was a useful
diversion if for any reason the main line through the centre of Ipswich
became unusable.

Cornhill–Lattice Barn
Via Major's Corner, Spring Road to Lattice Barn (junction of
Woodbridge Road), this tramway was laid with single track and passing loops from Spring Road/St. John's Road to Lattice Barn. There
was a stone viaduct over Spring Road and there was plenty of room
for the passage of cars.

71

Nos. 22 and 23 passing on the loop under the railway viaduct in Spring Road.

Cornhill–Bramford Road

Via Westgate Street, St. Matthew's Street, Barrack Corner, and thence single track with passing loops to Bramford Road railway bridge. Unfortunately, this bridge was too low to permit the passage of cars and was therefore the enforced terminus of the tramway in Bramford Road.

The map indicates the routes taken by the tramways. In conception the layout would appear to have been based on the idea of radial links from the Cornhill to the different parts of the borough, with the services providing cross-town facilities for intending passengers. At the outset, various service frequencies were tried on the tramways, but they soon settled down to be as follows:

Services operated on the tramways

Service	Frequency (minutes)
Ipswich railway station–Cornhill	7
Cornhill–Bourne Bridge	10
Bramford Road–Cornhill–Lattice Barn	10
Whitton–Cornhill–Derby Road	10

On weekdays the services commenced at 5.30 a.m. and operated until midnight; on Sundays the services started during the late morn-

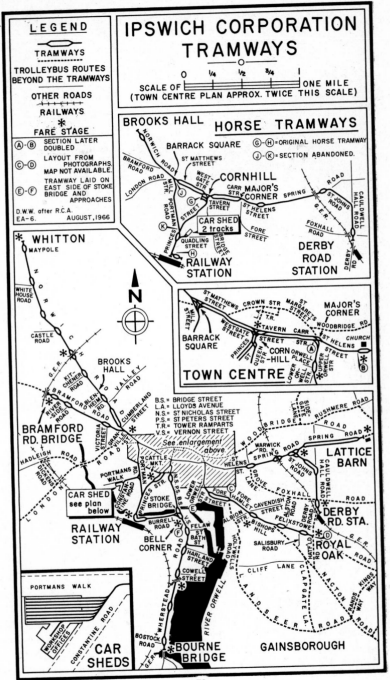

IPSWICH CORPORATION TRAMWAYS

SCALE OF |0 ¼ ½ ¾ 1| ONE MILE
(TOWN CENTRE PLAN APPROX. TWICE THIS SCALE)

LEGEND

— TRAMWAYS
TROLLEYBUS ROUTES BEYOND THE TRAMWAYS
OTHER ROADS
RAILWAYS
✳ FARE STAGE
(A)-(B) SECTION LATER DOUBLED
(C)-(D) LAYOUT FROM PHOTOGRAPHS. MAP NOT AVAILABLE.
(E)-(F) TRAMWAY LAID ON EAST SIDE OF STOKE BRIDGE AND APPROACHES

D.W.W. after R.C.A.
EA-6.   AUGUST, 1966

HORSE TRAMWAYS

BROOKS HALL
BARRACK SQUARE
(G)-(H) = ORIGINAL HORSE TRAMWAY
(J)-(K) = SECTION ABANDONED.

CORNHILL
MAJOR'S CORNER
CAR SHED 2 tracks
RAILWAY STATION
DERBY ROAD STATION

TOWN CENTRE

B.S. = BRIDGE STREET
L.A. = LLOYDS AVENUE
N.S. = ST NICHOLAS STREET
P.S. = ST PETERS STREET
T.R. = TOWER RAMPARTS
V.S. = VERNON STREET

MAJOR'S CORNER
BARRACK SQUARE
CORN-HILL

WHITTON
MAYPOLE
WHITE HOUSE ROAD
CASTLE ROAD
BROOKS HALL
BRAMFORD RD. BRIDGE
RAILWAY STATION
CAR SHED see plan below
STOKE BRIDGE
BELL CORNER
See enlargement above
CATTLE MKT.
PORTMANS WALK
PORTMANS WALK
CAR SHEDS
WORKSHOP OFFICES
BOURNE BRIDGE
GAINSBOROUGH
LATTICE BARN
DERBY RD. STA.
ROYAL OAK

N

73

A street scene of the tramway era; No. 36 at St. Helens, Ipswich.

Photo: Courtesy J. H. Price

ing. Average speed in service of the cars, based on running time and mileage, was six miles per hour; the maximum speed permitted by the Board of Trade was ten miles per hour.

Special services

Bath Street–Ipswich railway station

This service operated on occasions of the Great Eastern Railway steamer sailings from the Quay to Felixstowe Dock.

Derby Road railway station–various points in the borough

The extension into the railway station yard was used in connection with railway excursions to Felixstowe at Bank Holidays and other periods of similar heavy traffic.

Fares

These were based on mileage and were as follows:

1d. — up to 1.53 miles	
1½d. — up to 2.02 miles	
2d. — up to 3.04 miles	Average fare rate per mile = 0.693d.
2½d. — up to 3.54 miles	
3d. — up to 4.00 miles	

The tickets used were of the Bell Punch type, with pre-printed stages; they were cancelled by means of hand-operated punches. In addition to tickets issued on the cars by conductors, Ipswich Corpora-

74

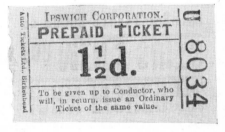

Specimen tickets of Ipswich Corporation.

75

tion also sold books of pre-paid tickets which had to be handed up at the time of travel to the conductor who, in return, issued an ordinary ticket of the same value.

Stopping places

These were fixed ; on single-track sections they were located at passing places and on the double-track sections at the main cross streets. Stops were defined as:

(a) Fare stage
(b) Cars stop if required
(c) All cars stop

On 14th September, 1904, cars were delayed throughout the borough for about three-quarters of an hour, owing to the breaking of a guard wire in the upper part of Princes Street. This wire fell on a "live" wire and the complete tramway service was stopped.

Half-fares were introduced on 10th August, 1905, for journeys taken before 8 a.m., but this had an extremely adverse effect on revenue, bringing the revenue per car mile down to 9d. However, various revisions were made to the fares and the position improved.

1914–1920

As with all tramway undertakings, the First World War affected the Ipswich undertaking in that, besides shortage of staff, raw materials and spare parts were, if not actually unobtainable, very difficult to obtain. Certain cars were painted grey (see schedule of cars) due to the difficulty of obtaining supplies of paint, and—perhaps more difficult to come by in the war years—skilled painters. It was during this war period that the disadvantage of laying tramways in narrow streets was really felt, as much heavy industrial traffic in connection with the war effort passed through the streets of Ipswich. As mentioned elsewhere in this book, it is much easier to pull a horse-drawn vehicle with metal-tyred wheels over metal rails than over macadam and, although motor vehicles were in evidence, horses were still the predominant prime movers, with the result that the rails of the tramways suffered great wear that was not due to the passage of tramway cars.

During the war—in 1917—the branch tramway along Bath Street, which had not been served for a number of years, was officially abandoned and the rails lifted. The poles remained, however, and were used to carry cables for the distribution of electricity to neighbouring houses. Ipswich used overhead cables rather than underground cables for the distribution of electricity to consumers, and much of the town is still thus supplied today.

1920–1931

At the end of the war the track was in a dangerous state, and in 1921, when rails again became available, the single-track section from Major's Corner to St. Helen's Church (about half a mile) was relaid with double track. The tramway in Norwich Road was also relaid at this time, but the track remained single. A short length of double track in Spring Road was relaid and this completed the work.

About 1922, the destination indicator boxes were removed and replaced by boards carried on the dashes. At the same time service numbers were introduced and were displayed on the cars by means of large illuminated boxes mounted on the upper deck rails at each end of the car, each service having a different coloured number.

Services operated at this time were as follows:

Service number	Indicator colour	Terminal points
1	Green	Whitton—Cornhill—Bourne Bridge
2	White	Bramford Road—Cornhill—Derby Road station
3	Blue	Ipswich railway station—Cornhill—Lattice Barn
4	Red	Ipswich railway station—Cornhill—Royal Oak

No. 28 at the terminus of route 4 at the Royal Oak Inn, showing the service number boards introduced in 1922.

77

A 1½d. minimum fare was introduced at about this time for two half-mile stages, but the 1d. fare remained for a single stage.

The next development came when the Corporation considered the future of the tramways and came to the conclusion that they would best be replaced by trolleybuses (or "trackless trams" as they were then known in the borough) because there was still a debt to pay off on the tramway system. As a result, in 1923, Ipswich Corporation decided that a Bill should be presented to Parliament to obtain powers to abandon the tramways and substitute trolleybuses.

The Corporation arranged to hire three trolleybuses from the Railless Company and on 2nd September, 1923, they commenced operating between the Cornhill and Ipswich railway station. As the chosen section was a tramway route, it was only necessary to erect a negative wire. In consequence, the tramways between Cornhill and Ipswich railway station, and in Portman Road between Princes Street and Mill Street, both fell into disuse. The three Railless/English Electric Company trolleybuses were 30-seat single-deck, pay-as-you-enter one-man-operated vehicles, with twin motors, and were numbered 1–3 in the Ipswich Corporation fleet. In view of the historical importance of these vehicles a detailed description of them is included at the end of this chapter.

The re-arranged services operated at follows:

Service No.	Terminal Points
1	Ipswich railway station—Cornhill (trolleybus)
2	Bramford Road—Cornhill—Derby Road railway station
3	Whitton—Cornhill—Lattice Barn
4	Royal Oak—Cornhill—Bourne Bridge

Unfortunately, neither the tramways nor the experimental trolleybuses were popular with the residents of Ipswich, and a large proportion of them preferred the idea of replacing the tramways by motor buses. However, the Corporation pressed on with their scheme and a fourth experimental trolley vehicle (a Ransomes, Sims and Jefferies 30-seat single-decker) was acquired in 1924. In the same year, the Eastern Counties Road Car Company Limited wrote to the Corporation and offered to provide a group of bus services in Ipswich, at the same time paying the Corporation £6,000 per year for 20 years, subject to the Corporation handing over their four experimental trolleybuses and giving the company adequate protection against competition.

The Council were not in favour of accepting the offer and early in 1925 held a referendum by which the ratepayers could indicate whether or not they wished the Corporation to promote their Bill in Parliament. The ratepayers voted in favour of trolleybuses by 3,780 votes to 2,156 votes, and as a result the Corporation went ahead with their promotion of the Bill. During 1925 another experimental trolley vehicle (a Tilling Stevens 30-seat single-decker) was purchased.

Although the Corporation's Bill did not receive the Royal Assent until 7th August, 1925, trolleybuses took over the tramway service to Bourne Bridge on 17th July, 1925. A final experimental vehicle followed in 1926 (a Ransomes 31-seat dual-entrance single-decker) and then quantity delivery of trolleybuses commenced, progressively replacing the tramways as follows:

To Royal Oak and beyond	27th May, 1926
To Lattice Barn and Derby Road station	9th June, 1926
To Whitton	27th July, 1926
To Bramford Road and beyond	27th July, 1926

The livery chosen for the trolleybuses was green and cream, with the Corporation's crest and the initials I.C.T. on the side panels. In later years, when double-deck trolleybuses were purchased, the vehicles had the unusual feature of having the lower-deck side panels unpainted; the panels were left in natural aluminium finish, the metal having a mechanically-etched decorative surface.

A. S. Black was the manager at the time of the final conversion to trolleybuses. He succeeded W. F. Ayton who, having managed the undertaking from the start of the tramways, had left the service of the Corporation in 1925 to become General Manager of Ransomes, Sims and Jefferies Limited.

The tramways had been replaced between May and July of 1926 (the last tram operating on the night of 26th July, 1926) by 15 Ransomes 31-seat single-deck dual-entrance trolleybuses, numbered 6–20, and 15 similar Garrett trolleybuses numbered 21–35. The final experimental vehicle (fleet No. 6—DX 5409) was withdrawn in 1926, its number being taken by another new vehicle of the initial production batch. The conversion, then, was accomplished with 35 trolleybuses which commenced to operate services over 13¼ route miles.

Over the next few years, the tramway rails were lifted (during which time the main streets were closed to traffic) with the exception of those outside the police station (near the Cornhill) which were covered over and still remain in position. However, as the trolleybuses at Ipswich were known as "trackless trams," with the often abbreviated use of the term as "trams," the identity of the tramways did not entirely disappear. Indeed, at Whitton, until the end of trolleybus operation, there was a cinder patch labelled "TRAM TURNING CIRCLE."

In 1929 certain extensions were made to the power station, with a view to increasing its capacity as a result of the increased demand for electricity.

Further extensions were made to the trolleybus services and between 1926 and 1931 ten additional 31-seat dual-entrance vehicles were acquired, all built by Ransomes, Sims and Jefferies Limited, except for No. 45, which was a Garrett with a 31-seat single-deck centre-entrance body.

1931–1950

Between 1931 and 1934 the remaining five experimental single-deck trolleybuses were withdrawn, and the first double-deck vehicles came in 1933. They were Ransomes, Sims and Jefferies chassis with Ransomes 48-seat bodies (24 seats on each deck), and numbered 46–49. They were followed between 1934 and 1936 by 17 similar vehicles. All were later re-seated to carry 26 passengers on the upper deck and 20 on the lower deck. In 1935, 53 vehicles were operating on 16.17 route miles.

The year 1936 saw the opening of a new depôt at Priory Heath, just off the Felixstowe Road. It was intended for trolleybuses only, and featured body repair and paint shops which were later used for the maintenance of motor bus bodies.

Further new trolleybuses were delivered between 1937 and 1940 and, although the chassis continued to be built by Ransomes, Sims and Jefferies, they carried double-deck bodies built by Massey Brothers of Wigan. Seating a total of 48 passengers (24 on each deck), they were numbered consecutively from 68 to 86. No. 86 was the last Ransomes trolleybus to be built and had been intended as a chassis demonstration vehicle for a proposed South African tour. Incidentally, the last Ransomes trolleybus to operate in this country was Ipswich Corporation No. 81, which was withdrawn after last running on 22nd March, 1958.

In 1942, 52 miles of overhead trolley line and 34 overhead trolley line junctions were renewed for carbon slipper operation (i.e. the trolley head carried a carbon "slipper" block as opposed to a revolving wheel for picking up power). Four Karrier W/English Electric Company

An Ipswich trolleybus turns at Whitton. Note the sign "Tram Turning Circle."

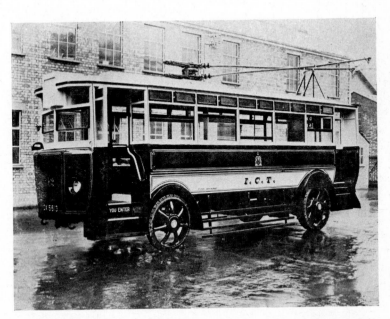

One of the first batch of trolleybuses delivered to Ipswich for tramway replacement. *Photo: Ransomes, Sims and Jefferies Ltd.*

F

vehicles with Weymann 56-seat "Austerity" bodies (30 seats upper deck, 26 lower deck) were acquired in 1944 and numbered 87–90, to be followed in 1945 by twelve Karrier W/Metropolitan-Vickers vehicles with "Austerity" Park Royal 56-seat bodies (30 seats upper deck, 26 lower deck). These last twelve were numbered 91–102.

By 1946 a number of earlier vehicles had been withdrawn and various route extensions had been made, resulting in the position that 57 double-deck trolleybuses and 17 single-deck trolleybuses were operating services over 23.44 route miles. At this time a number of extensions to the trolleybus network of services were being planned. In 1949 the re-routing in the centre of the town of eastbound trolley-buses increased the route mileage to 25.5 miles, which was the maximum trolleybus route mileage to be reached by Ipswich Corporation. The schedule opposite sets out the dates of opening of the various extensions.

The year 1948 saw the delivery of six more Karrier W/Metropolitan-Vickers Park Royal 56-seat trolleybuses, numbered 103–8, to be followed in 1949 by six Sunbeam F4/Metropolitan-Vickers Park Royal

One of the first double-deck Ipswich trolleybuses, as new in 1933.
Photo: Ransomes, Sims and Jefferies Ltd.

Routes opened for trolley vehicles

Cornhill and Ipswich station ...	2nd September, 1923*
,, ,, Bourne Bridge ...	17th July, 1925*
,, ,, Felixstowe Road (Kingsway) ...	27th May, 1926*
,, ,, Lattice Barn ...	9th June, 1926*
,, ,, Derby Road station ...	9th June, 1926*
,, ,, Whitton ...	27th July, 1926*
,, ,, Bramford Road ...	27th July, 1926*
,, ,, Foxhall Road ...	22nd December, 1926
,, ,, London Road (Ranelagh Road)	27th March, 1927
Derby Road, Royal Oak, Hatfield Road, Rands Circle ...	18th March, 1928
Cornhill and Gainsboro Estate ...	28th July, 1931
Lattice Barn and Rushmere Heath ...	25th April, 1934
Ranelagh Road to London Road Terminus	16th May, 1934
Hyde Park Corner to Electric House ...	6th December, 1936
Electric House, Woodbridge Road, Rushmere Road, Colchester Road, Heath Road, Bixley Road to Kingsway ...	6th December, 1936
Major's Corner and Mulberry Tree ...	6th December, 1936
Foxhall Road (Isolation) and Bixley Road/ Foxhall Road Junction ...	13th December, 1936
Reynolds Road and Holbrook Road, Landseer Road ...	30th January, 1938
Dickens Road and Hadleigh Road ...	31st October, 1938
Nacton Road (Randsway to Lindbergh Road), Lindbergh Road and Cobham Road ...	23rd April, 1939
Duke Street, Holywells Road to Holbrook Road ...	26th February, 1940
Clapgate Lane ...	17th December, 1945
Sidegate Lane ...	10th April, 1947
Nacton Road (Lindbergh Road to Airport)	17th August, 1947
Lloyds Avenue ...	10th July, 1949

* Ex-tramway routes

56-seat trolleybuses, numbered 109–14, and in 1950 by the last trolley-buses to be purchased by Ipswich Corporation, which were twelve Sunbeam F4/MV-Park Royal 56-seaters. The trolleybus fleet was now at its maximum with 81 double-deck and 17 single-deck vehicles.

1950–1963

In June, 1950, Alderman S. C. Grimwade of the County Borough of Ipswich officially opened the new Cliff Quay Generating Station.

The construction of the station had been started by the Ipswich County Borough Council and work was in progress when the British Electricity Authority (now the Central Electricity Generating Board) took over in 1948. The generating station, which has been in service since March, 1949, replaced the old power station at Constantine Road depôt.

Ipswich Corporation must be one of the last—if not the last—major municipal transport undertakings to commence motor bus operation, as it was not until May, 1950, that such vehicles started working on Ipswich Corporation services. The Corporation had decided that new transport facilities to housing estates should be provided by motor buses and, resulting from certain trolleybus route closures in the early 1950s and various other factors, it was eventually decided that the remaining trolleybuses should be gradually replaced by motor buses.

The motor buses, which are painted green and cream, are of both single- and double-deck types, with chassis manufactured by the Associated Equipment Company Limited and bodies by Park Royal Vehicles Limited.

Electric road passenger traction in Ipswich—and in East Anglia—ceased when on Friday, 23rd August, 1963, the last Ipswich Corporation trolleybus, No. 114, entered the depôt. Several of the more modern trolleybuses, Nos. 119–126 (ADX 189–196), were sold to Walsall Corporation for further service, and single-deck trolleybus No. 44, built in 1930 and withdrawn in 1953, was purchased by Mr. J. Cook who presented the vehicle on 1st July, 1955, to the British Transport Commission, who have placed the vehicle in the British Transport Museum at Clapham.

At the time of writing the motor bus fleet stood at 54 double-deck vehicles and eight single-deck vehicles.

Schedule of cars

1–26

Delivered for the opening of the tramways in 1903, these were double-deck open-top cars, with reversed staircases and three-window (per side) bodies, built by the Brush Electrical Engineering Company of Loughborough, and mounted on Brush trucks of Brill 21E pattern. The wheelbase was 6 ft., weight of car 10 tons, length 27 ft. 8 in. over collision fenders, over platforms 26 ft. 8 in.; inside body length 16 ft. 8 in., height inside 6 ft. 6 in. and width overall 5 ft. 9 in. and making the Ipswich cars the narrowest ever used in this country. The cars had seating for 28 persons outside and 22 inside. Braking equipment consisted of an electric rheostatic brake, hand wheel brake, and a hand track brake. Tidswell lifeguards and a pedal sand box completed the mechanical rigging.

Each car had electric bell pushes, and 16 electric lamps, six of which were used in the two illuminated destination indicator boxes, the backs of which carried an illuminated notice against smoking in front of the trolley stand, which was supplied by Brecknell, Munro and Rogers, Bristol. Motors and controllers were by Westinghouse, and automatic circuit breakers and magnetic cut-outs were provided. In addition to the destination boxes, there were side boards hung from the top deck rails, but these boards were at a later date fixed along the side of the decency screens at roof top height. There was an interesting notice on the cars which stated "GOLD COINS WILL NOT BE ACCEPTED IN PAYMENT OF FARE."

A feature of the cars was their "free springing" in that the leaf damper springs were not fixed to the car body at each end of the spring; the inner ends of the springs were tied to the side frame of the truck and this resulted in a much greater flexibility. When the track deteriorated there was too much flexibility!

27–36
Delivered in 1903, these cars were identical to the first batch of cars. There was also a car for watering and general purposes (builder unknown).

Livery
The cars were painted dark green and cream, outlined in gold and black, with the fleet number on each dash, the Corporation crest at the centre of the waist panel, and "Ipswich Corporation Tramways" on the rocker panel. During the First World War, ten cars (Nos. 2, 5, 15, 16, 17, 18, 21, 22, 31 and 36) were painted grey overall. The only car of the ten to be restored to its original green and cream livery was No. 36; the remainder stayed grey and were used on special work-people's services. After the First World War, as cars were repainted, the wording "Ipswich Corporation Tramways" was replaced by the initials I.C.T.

In 1919, Nos. 7 and 23 were withdrawn from service, but not scrapped until the abandonment of the tramways.

During 1922, the forward-facing destination indicator boxes were removed and replaced by large illuminated number boxes; the destination was displayed by means of a board carried on the dash.

Upon abandonment of the tramways, six of the cars were sold to the Scarborough Tramways Company, where they saw further service until that system was abandoned on 30th September, 1931. No. 34, minus its top deck and in its original livery, went to Felixstowe Pier. The Pier was demolished in 1949 and the body of 34 was also broken up. The remaining cars were sold locally.

Experimental trolleybuses Nos. 1–3

These vehicles were supplied on loan to Ipswich Corporation by Railless Limited (Short Brothers, a company owned by Railless Limited, built the bodies), and were single-deck vehicles with a seating capacity of 30 passengers each. Twenty-two passengers could be accommodated in the saloon, and a further eight passengers in an open-ended compartment at the rear end of the vehicle which was for the accommodation of smokers. The two compartments were separated by a sliding door.

The main passenger entrance to the vehicle was at the front, and was provided with a sliding door which was operated by means of a lever from the driver's compartment to facilitate one-man operation.

One of the experimental trolleybuses in Ipswich.

A pedestal-mounted ticket machine was installed at the front end of the vehicle.

The chassis was of the standard "Railless" two-motor type, and each rear road wheel was driven by a separate motor through a cardan shaft fitted with flexible couplings of the Hardy disc type. The steering gear was of the worm and nut type.

Each of the two English Electric Company D.K. 26B motors had a capacity of 20 b.h.p. at 525 volts on tramway rating at 1,000 revolutions per minute with full field. The controller, which consisted of a main and reversing barrel, was arranged to provide for forward and reverse running and for connecting the two motors in series or in parallel. There were various other refinements, including an interlocking device which was arranged so that the main barrel could not be moved from the "off" position unless the reversing barrel was in one of the operating positions, and the reversing barrel could not be moved unless the main barrel was on the "off" position.

Ticket machine (on trolleybuses 1–3)

This machine was an American product made by the Shanklin Rapid Transfer System, Springfield, Mass., and it was capable of issuing tickets at a rate of 60 per minute. The official Ipswich Corporation Tramways staff instruction issued at the time was as follows:

"The machine not only punches on the ticket the date, time, direction, leaving stage and price paid, but also sums up in pence the prices punched. The operator hands over his cash in accordance with this register at the end of the day. The machine is under the control of the motorman, and as each fare is paid he simply sets two buttons at the price paid and the stage number to which the passenger is entitled to ride, and operates a foot pedal. This automatically issues the ticket to the passenger. The date is locked in the rear of the machine, and is changed daily. The time is set with two small dials on the sides, which, together with the direction button, are changed at the end of each trip. The machine is small and compact, only weighing 21 pounds—and is mounted on a pedestal. The ticket is held by the passenger until leaving and is then given up to the motorman, so that he can check up to see that the passenger has not over-ridden. This arrangement not only gives the operator an absolute check on all passengers, but is also useful in making up traffic charts."

SHANKLIN RAPID TRANSFER SYSTEM, Springfield, Mass							
JAN	JUL	1	2	3	4	5	6
FEB	AUG.	7	8	9	10	11	12
MAR.	SEP.	13	14	15	16	17	18
APR.	OCT.	19	20	21	22	23	24
MAY	NOV.	25	26	27	28	29	30
JUN.	DEC.		UP	DOWN	31		

FARE	To Stage No.
1	1
$1\frac{1}{2}$	2
2	3
$2\frac{1}{2}$	4
3	5

DOG or LUGGAGE

TRANSFER

CHILD'S

WORKMAN'S

HOUR TIME											
1	2	3	4	5	6	7	8	9	10	11	12

A
M   P M | MINUTE TIME | 15 | 30 | 45 |

TICKET A.K.   389746

I.C.T.

See over for conditions of issue

A ticket issued by the American machine installed on the Ipswich experimental trolleybuses. (See previous page.)

88

CHAPTER FIVE

LOWESTOFT

Pre-1900

LOWESTOFT has for many years been an important fishing port, and this gave rise to the establishment of shipbuilding and repair yards, together with various ancillary industries, features which no doubt by reason of their similarity with Great Yarmouth, aroused interest in the minds of potential promoters of tramways. It was, of course, later that Lowestoft developed its other well-known aspect as a seaside resort.

The first proposal to construct tramways in Lowestoft came in 1882 when the Yarmouth and Gorleston Tramways Co. obtained powers to construct and work horse tramways within the borough of Lowestoft ; however, nothing came of this scheme.

The next proposal came in 1898 when, in August of that year, the Lowestoft Town Clerk received a letter from the East Anglian Light Railway Company (a subsidiary of the Drake and Gorham Electric Power and Traction Co. Ltd.) who wished to construct an electric light railway from Caister through Yarmouth and Lowestoft to Kessingland. The Council considered this proposal and on 11th October, 1898, agreed to support an application to the Light Railway Commissioners for sanction to construct the proposed tramway from Gorleston (junction with Yarmouth and Gorleston horse tramway) via Lowestoft to Kessingland, subject to the following clauses being inserted in the Light Railway Order:

(a) The Council to have power to purchase that part of the tramway within the Borough of Lowestoft at intervals of 7, 14, 21 or 28 years.

(b) The Council to receive a share of the profits over 10 per cent.

(c) The promoting company to take all the electricity required for the tramway south of Hopton from the Council's electricity works.

(d) The *whole* of the proposed tramway be opened in the stipulated time of three years from the commencement of the

Light Railway Order, if such be obtained by the promoting company.

The promoting company proceeded with its scheme, and in May, 1899, the Light Railway Commissioners held a public enquiry at the Town Hall, Lowestoft. At the hearing an objection was entered by the Great Eastern Railway and Great Northern Railway Joint Committee in respect of that part of the proposed tramway between Gorleston and Lowestoft, on the grounds that they already had powers for a railway covering the proposed Yarmouth and Lowestoft part of the tramway, and furthermore they were prepared to construct a tramway to Kessingland. As a result the Light Railway Commissioners refused to sanction that part of the tramway north of the swing bridge, but they recommended to the Board of Trade for confirmation that part of the tramway from the south side of the swing bridge (i.e. Royal Plain) to Kessingland, and these powers were granted in 1900 to the East Anglian Light Railway Company.

Upon being advised of the outcome of the hearing, the Council reconsidered the position and in July, 1899, decided that, in view of the new situation which had been brought about by the decision of the Light Railway Commissioners, it (the Council) was free to act on its own behalf and should obtain powers to construct and work under its own control an electric or other approved system of tramways within the borough of Lowestoft.

1900–1914

This decision of the Council was communicated to the East Anglian Light Railway Company who could not undertake to accept this proposal. Negotiations followed and various proposals and counter proposals were made by both parties, but eventually it was agreed that the Council should obtain powers for tramways within the borough, construct the tramways and lease them to the company. Accordingly the Council promoted a Bill which resulted in an Act of 1901 authorising the Council to construct various tramways within the borough.

After the Council had obtained the powers, the East Anglian Light Railway Company found it impossible to carry out the terms of the agreement and the Council then decided to construct and work the tramways itself. In 1904 the Council took over from the East Anglian Light Railway Company the powers for the southwards extension to Kessingland, but this tramway was not constructed.

Now that the Council had the powers to construct and work the proposed tramways the work of construction was put out to tender.

90

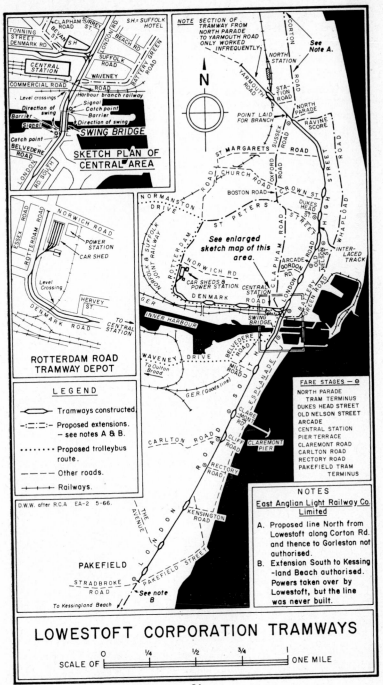

SKETCH PLAN OF CENTRAL AREA

ROTTERDAM ROAD TRAMWAY DEPOT

LEGEND

- ◇— Tramways constructed.
- -·⊏·⊐·⊏·- Proposed extensions.
  — see notes A & B.
- ········ Proposed trolleybus route.
- — — — Other roads.
- ┼─┼─┼─ Railways.

D.W.W. after R.C.A EA-2 5-66.

NOTE SECTION OF TRAMWAY FROM NORTH PARADE TO YARMOUTH ROAD ONLY WORKED INFREQUENTLY

See Note A.

See enlarged sketch map of this area.

FARE STAGES — ⊙

NORTH PARADE
TRAM TERMINUS
DUKES HEAD STREET
OLD NELSON STREET
ARCADE
CENTRAL STATION
PIER TERRACE
CLAREMONT ROAD
CARLTON ROAD
RECTORY ROAD
PAKEFIELD TRAM
        TERMINUS

NOTES

East Anglian Light Railway Co. Limited

A. Proposed line North from Lowestoft along Corton Rd. and thence to Gorleston not authorised.

B. Extension South to Kessing-land Beach authorised. Powers taken over by Lowestoft, but the line was never built.

LOWESTOFT CORPORATION TRAMWAYS

SCALE OF 0 ¼ ½ ¾ ONE MILE

These tenders covered the first part of the proposals, i.e. the north-south tramway, depôt access tramway, construction of depôt, supply of cars, and the ancillary equipment including extensions to the power station. The accepted tenders were as follows:

Alexander Penny and Co. of London (agents for the Société Anonyme de Marcinelle et Couillet, of Charleroi, Belgium, by whom the rails were rolled; Hadfield and Co., Sheffield, who did the special work in manganese steel for the junctions, points and crossings; Cooper and Howard Smith, who supplied the anchor and intermediate track joints) for supply of rails, fishplates and bolts — £6,053

George Wimpey and Co., Hammersmith, road contractors, for laying rails — £33,136

Robert W. Blackwell and Co., London—poles and overhead line equipment — £3,860

Callender's Cable Co.—underground feeder cables from electricity works to the tramways — £3,324

Westinghouse Electric and Manufacturing Co.—cars — £8,661

Brecknell, Munro and Rogers—special works car — £740

Musgrave and Sons, Bolton—boiler — £1,655

British Thomson-Houston Co.—switchboard — £750

British Thomson-Houston Co.—steam generator (Willans engine) — £4,200

Bertrams Ltd., Manchester—cooling condenser — £2,091

Babcock and Wilcox, London—pipework — £851

A. G. Beckett—buildings — £5,123

C. R. Cole—offices — £1,475

There was a long delay in the delivery of the rails, which eventually arrived in Lowestoft in the early hours of 10th March, 1903. The rails had been loaded into a sailing barge in Antwerp, and the barge was towed across the North Sea by a German tug. With a view to getting the tramways into operation for the summer season a very considerable bonus had to be offered to the permanent way contractors to persuade them to reduce their contract time by one half. However, there was no delay in getting the work of track laying underway, and the next day—11th March, 1903—the first rail was laid.

This event was accorded some ceremony. The Mayor issued invitations to various persons to attend the inaugural track laying at which a large number of local residents were also present, in addition to the Mayoress, members of the Town Council and the invited guests. The Mayoress, Mrs. Lancelot Orde, fixed the first copper rail bond on the first joint in the rails at the junction of London Road and Pakefield Street.

Mr. Hawtayne, the Council's consulting engineer, was ill and unable to be present, but his assistant, Mr. Zeden, presented the Mayoress with a souvenir on Hawtayne's behalf. This souvenir was in the shape of a paper weight with a silver model of the tramway track on a granite bed, and the model was housed in a case. The inscription on it was:

"Presented to the Mayoress (Mrs. Lancelot Orde) on the occasion of the laying of the first rail of the Lowestoft Corporation Tramways, March 11th, 1903."

After the presentation of the souvenir the Mayoress fixed the bond. The Mayor wound up the proceedings, and during his speech mentioned in humorous mood the delay in the supply of the rails which meant that work would have to proceed by day and night to get the tramways operating—he hoped that the residents in the High Street would not be too upset if they lost some sleep as a result of the night work. The Mayor stressed the need to get the tramways finished, as the sooner this was accomplished the sooner some money would be earned to help pay for the cost of constructing the tramways.

Work proceeded on the tramway which was mainly single track with passing places ; the route was just over four miles—one and one-third miles were double-track. There was a short length of interlaced track in High Street which was later relaid with ordinary single track. The gauge was 3 ft. 6 in. Necessary road improvements and widening of streets proved to be a major task, the claims alone amounting to £25,000, but after each claim had been examined on its merits the final amount was £14,000. The Corporation electricity works were opened in 1901 with a capacity of 225 kilowatts, but fortunately the works had been designed for extensions, which were made in 1903. These improvements and additional facilities increased the plant capacity to 1,575 kilowatts, or about 1,900 kilowatts on emergency load.

The same steam-raising plant was used for the electric lighting and the traction plant, although to cater for the additional current requirements one big Musgrave boiler of the marine dry back type was installed in addition to the four Babcock and Wilcox boilers. Superheaters were provided on the large boiler and two of the smaller boilers. The generating sets were chiefly by the British Thomson-Houston Co., who in conjunction with the British Westinghouse Co. supplied the balancers and boosters. There were two switchboards and two galleries. The cables from the electricity works to the tramway were laid by Callenders Cable Company.

The depôt was built in red brick with stone facings by the firm of A. G. Beckett of Oulton Broad to the design of J. Roberts of Lowestoft who was appointed architect under Hawtayne. The depôt could accommodate 16 cars and had four tracks, each with full-length inspection pit. A fifth track to a small shed at right-angles to the main depôt was added at a later date. Facilities were provided for repairs, carpenter's machine, fitters, paint shops and a smithy, together with accommodation for motormen and conductors. Viewed now, the depôt

Lowestoft depôt prior to the opening of the tramways, showing cars being assembled.   'Tramway and Railway World'

appears to have been sited far away from the north-south route but it formed part of the scheme for the more comprehensive system of tramways which did not materialise. The depôt access tramway did in fact continue for a short distance along Rotterdam Road to a point near its junction with Norwich Road.

The gradients on the tramway were negligible (the maximum was 1 in 27) and although the road widening mentioned above was necessary, the only other major work involved was the harbour bridge and this was a task which might have deterred many engineers. However, the problem was tackled with imagination, and the 40-ft. swing bridge erected in 1897 by the Great Eastern Railway was laid with a double-track tramway using rails with a special shallow section. The bridge (which is still in use at the time of writing in 1962) is worked by hydraulic power and on opening is first tilted and then swung upon a pivot; the tramway overhead line equipment was constructed so that it swung with the bridge as one unit. A device was incorporated so that when the bridge was tilted ready for opening the overhead line on the bridge and for some distance each side of the bridge automatically became dead. As further protection catch points were automatically set to derail any approaching car, and barriers were also placed across the road. Railway-type signals, which interlocked with the bridge mechanism, were provided each side of the bridge and all these safety devices meant that no car could approach the bridge when open. When the tramway was laid some difficulty was experienced in arranging for the carrying of the feeder cables under the harbour. The Council first invited tenders for the work but thought the lowest too high and eventually undertook the work itself to the directions of G. A. Bruce—doing the job for a quarter of the lowest tendered amount. The bridge is now owned by the British Railways Board.

The rails of the tramway were of the usual girder type, weighed 100 lb. to the yard and were 60 ft. in length; anchor and intermediate joints were used throughout. The rails were not welded at the joints, and the electrical bonding was completed by copper joints from rail to rail. Points at passing places and intersections were 12 ft. 3 in. long and of 96 ft. radius; crossings were 3 ft. 6in. long, with an angle of 1 in 6; depôt points were 6 ft. 6 in. long, with a radius of 42 ft.

The special work where the tramway crossed the dock railway in Waveney Road was by Hadfield and Co., as was that for the depôt fans, passing places and special junctions. The paving adopted consisted of basaltic lava and granite blocks laid on a bed of concrete six inches deep and grouted in with bitumen and cement. The basaltic lava blocks were laid between the rails; but on the edge next to the macadam, granite blocks were used. The following are a few approximate figures which give some idea of the amount of work involved in track laying for a comparatively small tramway undertaking. Total excavation amounted to about 12,000 cubic yards, and the resulting track bed was laid with 5,000 cubic yards of concrete. The tonnage of basaltic lava setts was 4,000, and 800 of granite setts; 900 tons of rails were used, and to bolt them together 35 tons of fishplates were required; 4.500 bonds were used throughout the tramway.

Two hundred and fifteen steel tubular poles with ornamental cast iron bases at approximately 40-yard intervals and, generally, tubular bracket arms, were used to support the overhead line which was of hard drawn copper of 30 S.W.G. (0.372-inch in diameter), weighing approximately 1,260 lb. per 1,000 yards; the overhead line was supported at a height of 21 feet above the road. Span wires and poles were used between the G.P.O. and the swing bridge, over the interlaced line beside the Triangle (Market Place), and on the depôt line at the junction of Denmark Road and Rotterdam Road. Stop signs were of white enamelled metal plates edged and lettered blue, and were lettered as follows: "All Cars Stop Here," "Cars Stop Here Going Up," "Cars Stop Here Going Down," and "Cars Stop Here If Requested." "Up" was northbound and "down" southbound. Small circular shelters built around an overhead pole were provided at each terminus and at Royal Plain.

For the opening of the tramways 15 cars were delivered; Nos. 1–11 were four-wheel open-top double-deck cars and Nos. 21–24 bogie single-deck cars. (See schedule of cars.)

Early in July, 1903, various tests were made and the cars were given trial trips at night over the tramways, disturbing the sleep of residents who lived on the line of the route. However, this was all to good purpose and the system was quickly made ready for inspection by the representatives of the Board of Trade. The overhead line equipment was inspected on Thursday, 16th July, by Mr. Trotter of the Board of Trade and it was arranged that the permanent way and cars would be inspected on Saturday, 18th July. There was some delay, however, and it was not until Tuesday, 21st July, that Colonel Van Donop made the final Board of Trade inspection. The Colonel was accompanied by the Mayor, Councillor L. F. Orde (who was also chairman of the Tramways Committee), and by representatives of the contractors when he travelled on a car over the system which, at the end of the inspection, he declared to be in order for public service.

The opening scene on the Lowestoft tramways on 22nd July, 1903.
'Tramway and Railway World'

On the following day, Wednesday, 22nd July, 1903, the inaugural opening ceremony took place and many people turned out to line the gaily-decorated route for the inaugural drive. The official party consisted of the Mayor, the Mayoress, members of the Council, representatives of the contractors, the technical and local Press, and invited guests. This party met at the tramway depôt at 11.30 a.m. and after the crews had been lined up for inspection by the Mayor, the party inspected the depôt. The first car—a double-decker—left the depôt shortly before 12.15 p.m. and this car was decorated overall with flags and evergreens and festoons of flowers around the windows. The Mayor drove this car which also conveyed his private friends, Aldermen and their ladies. Another double-deck car followed with members of the Council as its passengers, and in third place was a single-deck car provided for the engineers and contractors; the fourth car conveyed representatives of the Press, and the fifth the invited guests. The procession of cars went first to the northern terminus, then to the southern terminus, and so back to the Grand Hotel where the party alighted for the official lunch.

The cars then operated for public service, and a large number of people took the opportunity of riding on the tramway on the opening

G

day. At this time a 1d. universal fare was charged. A seven-minute service was operated, and the average speed was 5.61 m.p.h.

The tramway ran from Yarmouth Road (the borough boundary) in the north, via High Street, London Road North, Swing Bridge, London Road South, to the terminus at Pakefield. From the main tramway there was a depôt-access tramway along Denmark Road to the depôt in Rotterdam Road. Other tramways were proposed (see map) and authorised but none were built; actually 4.08 route miles were built and a further 3.82 miles were authorised but not built. An interesting feature of the tramway was the short stretch of interlaced track near the Triangle.

Cars were operated for about three weeks after the opening between Belle Vue Park and the depôt but this service was withdrawn through lack of patronage. After this withdrawal passengers were conveyed on any car which was proceeding to or from the depôt. The overhead line frogs were removed at the triangular junction near Central Station and cars from the north turning into Denmark Road were driven as far round as possible until the trolley pulled off the overhead line. In fact, to make this movement, the trolley had to be rewired twice, and this also applied to cars from the depôt switching to the south-bound line.

The cost of the tramway undertaking, including the compensation for street widening, was £90,000, and it is interesting to note that in the first fourteen days of operation the undertaking carried 165,900 passengers and took £792.

In 1904 four more double-deck cars, numbered 12–15, were purchased (see schedule of cars).

Some trouble was experienced with the road bed and the foundations, and temporary repairs cost £1,046 in 1909 and £1,479 in 1910. The portion of the tramway north of the railway bridge at Lowestoft North station was premature and by about 1910 the service terminated at North Parade. The same year, 1910, saw a revision in fares; the through 1d. fare was increased to 2d. and two 1d. stages were introduced—North Parade to Pier Terrace and Central Station to Pakefield. Further trouble was experienced with the track and in 1911 a further £1,726 was spent in temporary repairs. However, it was necessary to do more than temporary repair work as the foundations in many places were more or less rotten and the basaltic lava blocks were wearing away. In February, 1912, the Council decided to spend £10,000 on a

Car No. 11 in London Road, Pakefield.

No. 2 on the interlaced track near the Triangle, Lowestoft.

thorough renovation of the track and accordingly the money was borrowed, to be repaid over a period of fifteen years.

By 1913, when H. H. Saunders took over the management from G. A. Bruce, there was an accumulated deficit of £26,000. At about this time a consultant was engaged to enquire into the operation of the tramways and as a result of his report fares were then raised by almost 50 per cent to 0.83d. per mile; after that the small undertaking proved profitable. The fares introduced in 1913 were as follows:

North Parade—Arcade
Dukes Head Street—Central Station
Old Nelson Street—Pier Terrace
Central Station—Claremont Road   1d.—Green tickets
Pier Terrace—Rectory Road
Carlton Road—Pakefield
Central Station—Depôt

North Parade—Pier Terrace
Dukes Head Street—Claremont Road
Old Nelson Street—Rectory Road   2d.—Blue tickets
Central Station—Pakefield

North Parade—Pakefield   3d.—Pink tickets

Scholars' tickets $\frac{1}{2}$d.—White tickets

Children, workmen and luggage   1d.—(any distance)

Local police, sailors and United
    Automobile (later Eastern Counties)
    employees free.

It is worth recording that the fares as set in 1913 lasted right into the bus era and until after the 1939–45 war.

1914–1931

During the First World War, and in particular during 1917 and 1918, the undertaking employed women drivers, conductors and inspectors in an effort to meet the shortage of male staff caused by con-

scription into the armed forces. As was the case with other tramway undertakings, raw materials for maintenance were in short supply—often they were impossible to obtain—and many difficulties resulted from this situation.

After the war the tramway appears to have had a quiet life but certain notable incidents are worth recording. It seems that the undertaking had two amusing encounters with animals; for instance, a circus promoter called to see the tramways manager with a request that a baby elephant be conveyed from Pakefield to the town centre. The manager agreed to this, the floor of a car was strengthened and the elephant conveyed for the appropriate adult single fare of 2d.!

Perhaps more amusing was the "incident of the dancing bear." This occurred before the First World War and concerned a car operating a normal service journey. As the car approached a stop, an Italian circus master was waiting there with a dancing bear. The conductor was not keen on having the bear in the car but after consulting with the driver—who said that the bear was in the same category as a dog—the bear was allowed on the car and the Italian took it on the top deck. This caused great consternation to the other passengers seated on the top deck and they promptly disappeared down the front stairs. The bear and dancing master were left alone, so to keep the bear amused the dancing master struck up a tune on his concertina and the bear began to prance about on the top deck.

Passengers waiting at stops on the line of route stared in amazement at this sight and refused to board the car, but at the Central Station the Italian alighted complete wth bear and no trouble was caused. Although action was considered against the staff concerned, none was taken, but an instruction was given to the effect that no bears were to be allowed to travel on the cars!

On one occasion a car was used in connection with a wedding, and the bridal party travelled on the hired car from St. Peter's Road to St. John's Church. At various times cars were decorated for use at carnivals, and one was decorated as a "Chinese Pagoda." The tramways manager H. H. Saunders and his family made the many thousands of paper blooms with which the "Pagoda" was covered. This car ran in the Carnival of 1924 and at night was a mass of pink light; passengers were carried and a fare of 6d. was charged.

Discipline was strict, and much emphasis was put on good time-keeping. Each car was fitted with a clock, and incorrect time meant seven days' suspension from duty without pay. Delay was experienced by the opening of the swing bridge, and quite how the timekeeping question was resolved is not recorded.

In 1920 the Corporation obtained power to operate trolleybuses and motor buses, but the first buses were not acquired until 1927. The trolleybus route is of interest in that it was proposed to serve new areas, including Oulton, for which tramway powers had not been obtained. Poles and span wires were erected along Rotterdam Road and part of Normanston Drive in anticipation of trolleybus operation, but no overhead line was erected. When the decision was taken not to introduce trolleybuses the span wires were used to support lamps for overhead street lighting. The particular roads over which the proposed trolleybus service was routed were served by buses of the United Automobile Co. Ltd. (now the Eastern Counties Omnibus Co. Ltd.), and this may have had something to do with the decision not to proceed with the introduction of trolleybuses.

If trolleybuses had been introduced it is a matter for speculation as to whether the trams would have been replaced by trolleybuses and not motor buses as was the case.

Bus operation commenced in 1927 when two Guy 20-seater single-deck buses (Nos. 1 and 2) were delivered for the "Sea Wall" service; this was operated during the summer only on a "one-man-bus" basis. (See reproduction of notice on next page.) Fares on this service were:

Full Circular Tour 6d. (yellow ticket)
Between South Pier and North Parade 3d. (white ticket)
Between Sea Wall and North Parade 1d. (light blue ticket)
Between South Pier and Hamilton Road 1d. (ditto)

The "Sea Wall" service operated every summer until 1939, by which time the starting point was at Kensington Gardens. The fares were then as follows:

Kensington Gardens to Royal Plain	1d.
Royal Plain to Hamilton Road	1d.
Hamilton Road to Sea Wall	1d.
Sea Wall to North Parade	1d.
Kensington Gardens or Royal Plain to North Parade	3d.
Circular Tour ticket	6d.

MOTOR OMNIBUS
SERVICE

WILL RUN DAILY

By the SILVERY SEA

OPEN SALOON OMNIBUSES will leave the SOUTH PIER at half-hour intervals for a SEASIDE TOUR along the Sea Wall, past the Bathing Pool, Tennis Courts and Recreation Ground, Sparrow's Nest and Belle Vue Park, to North Parade, near the Golf Course and return, covering a delightful SEASIDE DRIVE of nearly six miles.

FARES

Full Circular Tour - - - - - -	6d.
Between South Pier & North Parade -	3d.
,, Sea Wall & North Parade -	1d.
,, South Pier & Hamilton Road -	1d.

DAILY FROM 11 a.m. TILL DUSK.

Passengers can join the Buses at any point of the Route for the Circular Tour.

Saloon Buses will run from inside the Sparrow's Nest Gardens at the end of the Evening Performances.

Flood & Son, Ltd., The Borough Press, Lowestoft.

In 1928 three similar Guy vehicles (Nos. 3–5), but with increased seating to carry 26 passengers, were delivered to the Corporation and commenced work on a service from St. Peter's Street (Beccles Road)/ Cemetery Corner via Beccles Road (now part of St. Peter's Street), St. Peter's Street, Triangle, High Street, Old Nelson Street, Battery Green, Waveney Road, Central Station, Bevan Street, Maidstone Road, Selby Street, and back to Norwich Road (Rotterdam Road, tramway offices).

Fares

Norwich Road (tramway offices) to Old Nelson Street
Old Nelson Street to Central Station $\left.\rule{0mm}{10mm}\right\}$ 1d. stages
Central Station to Norwich Road

No special tickets were printed; the ordinary 1d. tramway tickets were used. The half-hourly service was operated by two buses, one operating in each direction around the route. It continued for several months until it was withdrawn because of its unremunerative nature. The reason for the service not being a circular one was that the then United Automobile Services Ltd. had a protection over that particular stretch of Rotterdam Road between Norwich Road corner and the Cemetery Corner on their Lowestoft–Oulton Broad service.

The year 1929 saw the introduction of a half-hourly bus service along the tramway route but extended to the North Boundary. As the fares remained at those on the tramway service it was a long penny ride to the North Boundary terminus. Despite statements to the contrary it appears that the tramway from North Parade along Yarmouth Road to the North Boundary was intact until the abandonment of the tramway, as cars now ran over this section on school days to serve the Grammar School; one car reached the school in the morning at about 8.45 a.m. and a car left the school just after 12 noon, returning there about 1.15 p.m.

By 1930 the tramway was approaching the end of its useful life and the decision whether to re-equip the line and make certain extensions, or to abandon it and replace by motor buses, had to be made. It was decided to adopt the latter course and the Electricity and Transport Committee made application to the Ministry of Transport for a grant towards removal of the tramway and making up the roadway. However, the Ministry of Transport preferred some alternative method of financing the work and so an application was made to the Unemployment Grants Committee for a grant to assist with the work.

On 8th April, 1931, the Town Clerk reported that the Unemployment Grants Committee was prepared to give a grant of 75 per cent of the wages bill provided that unemployed men were taken on for the work. The Council agreed to this and, as Ministry sanction had been received for the road works, the Surveyor was authorised to commence removal of the rails, which commenced on Friday, 10th April, 1931, and had to be completed within three months. The Ministry of Transport had given formal sanction to the borrowing by the Council of £16,741 for the provision of twelve buses (eight double-deck and four single-deck); the loan was repayable over eight years. The single-deck vehicles came first and were used as mentioned above.

In 1931 four 34-seat Guy single-deck buses (numbered 6–9) were purchased and operated together with buses Nos. 1–5 on tramway feeder services while the track was being lifted—but this is anticipating the end of the tramways.

The tramway was split into two sections; that part from the swing bridge to the North Boundary was lifted first and the service maintained by buses which connected at the swing bridge with the trams which continued to work on the southern section to Pakefield. The remaining new buses—A.E.C. "Regents" with petrol engines and "United" double-deck bodies seating 47 passengers—were ready for service at the beginning of May, 1931, and the last tram ran on 8th May, 1931.

On 8th May, 1931, the last car was driven by the oldest driver who had been employed by the Corporation since the tramway undertaking opened in 1903. The car carried a huge wreath of arum lilies heavily bordered and crossed with black; crowds of people turned out and the trams were stripped of bells, indicators and other items by souvenir hunters.

The next day buses took over the service and the rails were progressively lifted, those over the swing bridge being taken up at night. A number of the overhead standards were removed to other parts of the borough for lighting purposes and do not form a reliable guide to the old tramway routes. Saunders remained with the undertaking until 30th June, 1945.

In the 28 years of operation, 80,000,000 passengers were conveyed and car mileage was 8,000,000 miles—ten passengers carried for every mile run!

106

Car No. 2 in the depôt yard with a newly-delivered Guy FC bus in 1931.
Photo: Courtesy A. V. Bird

The last car working in service on the final day of tramway operation in
Lowestoft, 8th May, 1931.   *Photo: Courtesy A. V. Bird*

A glimpse of the "last car" after it had been stripped by souvenir hunters.

The depôt at Rotterdam Road is still used for Corporation buses, but at the time of writing (1962) the track remains in the yard although that inside has been covered. The small shed at the depôt was used to house a 1916 ex-R.A.F. Thornycroft breakdown tender; this vehicle still exists.

Schedule of cars

All the cars were supplied by the British Westinghouse Electric and Manufacturing Co.

No. 6 as new; note the smart uniform of driver and conductor.

Double-deck cars 1–11

Bodies were built by G. F. Milnes & Co. and each body was mounted on a Milnes truck. They had seating for 48 passengers (22 inside and 26 outside) and had reversible-back wooden seats on the top deck and longitudinal seats covered with rugs on the lower deck. Overall length was 33 ft. 6 in., width 6 ft. 7 in., and there were four drop windows each side. These cars were known as "summer cars" (but were used all the year round). The safety fence on the top deck was of ornamental ironwork instead of the more usual wire mesh. Two Westinghouse type 46 25 h.p. motors and offset trolley standards completed the general layout.

Double-deck cars 12–15

Identical to Nos. 1–11 except that they had Westinghouse type 90 motors and type 46 controllers.

Single-deck cars 21–24 with clerestory roofs

Bodies built by G. F. Milnes & Co. and each body mounted on a pair of Milnes maximum-traction trucks. The bodies consisted of three sections with a six-window closed central compartment and an open smoking compartment at each end. On one side of the smoking compartment there was an ornamental metal grill, but at the other side the panelling was carried right along to the bulkhead in the usual manner. Transverse garden seating for 38 passengers was installed in the central compartment, and six seats in each smoking compartment. Although known as "winter cars" these cars were occasionally used during the summer and were the only bogie cars to operate on any East Anglian tramway system. Wire-mesh guards were fitted between the trucks after an accident when a child was run over.

Standard equipment was 16 interior lamps, each with a fancy shade (double-deck cars had a roof light at each end of the top deck), collapsible gates on platforms, lifeguards of the Tideswell type, illuminated roller blind destination indicators, and electric bells. The destination boxes were removed after the First World War, but small boards (painted yellow with red lettering) on the side of the cars listed the principal places of interest along the line of route. At one period Lowestoft cars carried a letter box on the dash.

The wooden interior seats were covered with rugs monogrammed with the initials of the Council, the woodwork was finished in polished maple, and the glass ventilation lights over the main windows carried coloured transfer advertisements for local traders. The livery of the cars was Tuscan red and primrose lined out in gold, the coat of arms of the borough being displayed on the rocker panels, and the lettering and numbers gold shaded blue and silver. Other fitments were brass rails, interior curtains of old gold, and ornamental wood panelled ceiling. The trucks and lifeguards were painted red.

Westinghouse standard electrical equipment (i.e. car controllers, series/parallel with magnetic blow-out, canopy switches, lightning arresters and automatic circuit breakers) and two Westinghouse type 46 25 h.p. motors were installed in all cars (except 12–15, see above). All cars had hand-operated wheel brakes and hand-operated track brake, together with a rheostatic brake operated from the controller.

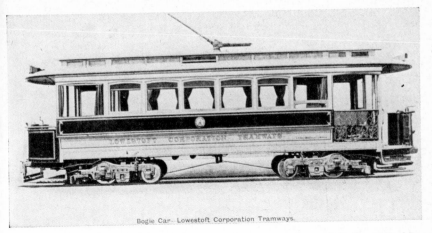

A side view of one of the single-deckers. *Photo: 'Tramway and Railway World'*

Seen on the last day of operation is car No. 14, now preserved at the East
Anglia Transport Museum.   *Photo: Courtesy A. V. Bird*

The Lowestoft Corporation works car of 1903.

In addition to these cars there was a special car mounted on Brush reversed maximum-traction trucks. It was supplied by Messrs. Brecknell, Munro and Rogers and was used for sprinkling, sweeping and generally scavenging the track. This car was painted French grey and lettered black, but had no number.

All the cars survived until the closing of the system, and a few bodies can still be seen in the district but in derelict condition with the exception of No. 14 which is being restored at the East Anglia Transport Museum, Carlton Colville, near Lowestoft.

Schedule of buses in operation at time of conversion from trams to buses

Fleet No.	Registration No.	Chassis	Body	Seating capacity	Delivered
1–2	RT3426/5	Guy BB	Waveney	20	1927
3–5	RT4656–8	Guy BB	Waveney	26	1928
6–9	RT7719–22	Guy FC	United	34	1931
10–17	RT7723–30	AEC "Regent"	United	27 upper 20 lower	1931

The first buses were lettered "Lowestoft Corporation Tramways" on the waist-band but tickets were headed "Lowestoft Corporation Motors." When the tramways were abandoned the buses were lettered

"Lowestoft Corporation Transport," the livery remaining the same as on the cars until 1938 when the present maroon and primrose livery was introduced.

One of the A.E.C. double-decker replacement buses.
Photo: R. W. Gamble

H

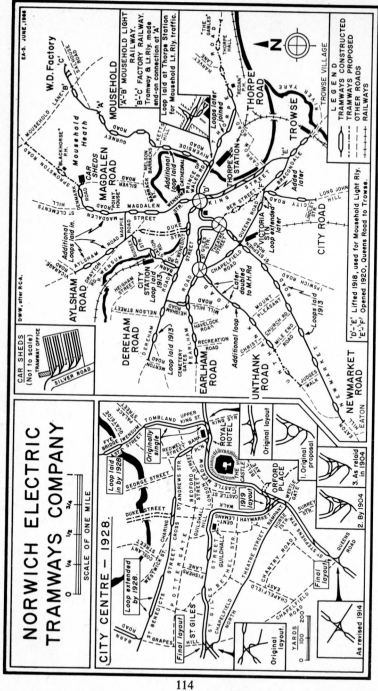

CHAPTER SIX

NORWICH

IT would be quite unwise to attempt to describe in detail in a book of this nature the development of the city of Norwich and, in any event, there are many books readily available on the subject. Some background knowledge is, however, desirable to appreciate the development of tramways in the city.

Only 30 years after the Conquest, Herbert de Losinga, the first Bishop of Norwich, founded the cathedral which despite alterations and additions still stands and provides one of the best examples of Norman architecture in this country. Over the years the city has developed and, in 1801, with a population of 37,000 people, it was the eighth largest town of England. Standing on a large mound in the centre of the city is the great Norman keep of Norwich Castle.

Complementary to the expansion in population has been the growth of trade and industry, and by the nineteenth century Norwich had become an important centre for the manufacture of mustard, shoes and silk. Also established were breweries and printers.

As capital of the county of Norfolk, the city transacted considerable business, and it is perhaps rather surprising that the introduction of railed street transport came so late when the examples at Cambridge, Great Yarmouth and Ipswich are considered.

The first recorded instance of public transport in Norwich is early in the nineteenth century when a sedan chair plied for hire in Devil's Alley (now Opie Street), but although a horse tramway was laid down and opened for traffic in Great Yarmouth on 1st April, 1875, a tramway was not opened in Norwich until the end of the nineteenth century, despite the fact that several schemes were promoted or suggested in the intervening years. In 1864 an Act of Parliament was obtained for a proposed Wensum Valley Railway, and although the scheme was abandoned it gave rise to a proposal by the East Norfolk Tramway Company Limited for a standard-gauge horse tramway linking Norwich with Costessey and Taverham. The tramway was to have run from Norwich, Thorpe railway station, via Riverside Road, Pockthorpe Street, Bull Close Road, Magpie Road, Aylsham Road, Drayton Road, and thence via its own right of way to Hellesdon, Costessey and Taverham Paper Mills. When the proposals were considered by the Norwich City Council in August, 1870, it was stated that the tramway would prove useful for conveying the produce of several mills in the district (i.e. at Costessey and Taverham) to Norwich, besides catering for passengers. Norwich City Council agreed to support the scheme and in 1871 a Bill was promoted in Parliament for authorisation to construct the tramway, which was to have had 8.5 miles of track with an estimated cost of £14,000 for the construction work.

In January, 1872, at a further meeting of the Norwich City Council, it was announced that the Norwich, Costessey and Taverham tramway scheme was being considered by the Board of Trade, the necessary preliminaries having been complied with to the Board's satisfaction. However, no powers were obtained, and the scheme fell through.

The next development came in November, 1878, when the Provincial Tramways Company applied for permission to construct tramways in the city. The proposed route was from the Cemetery (Earlham) via Dereham Road, St. Giles Road, Chapel Field Road, Queens Road, Upper Surrey Street, All Saints Green, Golden Ball Street, Castle Meadow, Prince of Wales Road, Foundry Bridge and Thorpe Road to Whitlingham railway station. At an adjourned meeting of the City Council, held on 17th December, 1878, it was agreed not to oppose the Bill, subject to certain conditions, clauses and by-laws being incorporated in the proposed Bill. Agreement was reached between the City Council and the promoters and as a result the Norwich Tramways Bill was considered by a Select Committee of the House of Commons on 6th May, 1879. The Bill was opposed by the Great Eastern Railway Company and a Mr. Foster, a local resident, and was thrown out after only the promoters' case had been heard.

This proposed tramway, however, appeared to stimulate interest in public transport, as a company known as the Norwich Omnibus Company (not to be confused with the company formed in 1935) commenced operating a group of horse-drawn bus services. The first service commenced on 23rd June, 1879, between Thorpe railway station and Dereham Road. Other services were as follows:

Newmarket Road (Christchurch Road)—Market Place—Catton (Whalebone public house)

Unthank Road (Christchurch Road)—Market Place—Bracondale
(Ice House Lane)
Earlham Road (College Road)—Market Place—Thorpe Village

Certain revisions were made to the services from time to time and the timetable for the summer of 1883 gives the position which existed until horse bus operation ceased.

TIME TABLE OF THE NORWICH OMNIBUS COMPANY, LIMITED.

FROM	TO THE MARKET PLACE.
NEWMARKET RD.	8 45 9 15 9 45 10 15 10 45 11 15 11 45 12 15 12 45 1 15 1 45 2 15 2 45 3 15 3 45 4 15 4 45 5 15 5 45 6 15 6 45 7 15 7 45 8 15 8 45 ...
N.CATTON { Pitt St.	8 45 ... 9 45 ... 10 45 ... 11 45 ... 12 45 ... 1 45 ... 2 15 ... 3 15 ... 4 15 ... 5 15 ... 6 15 ... 7 15 ... 8 15 ... 9 15
{ Mag.St	... 9 15 ... 10 15 ... 11 15 ... 12 15 ... 1 15 ... 2 15 ... 3 15 ... 4 15 ... 5 15 ... 6 15 ... 7 15 ... 8 15 ... 9 15
DEREHAM ROAD	8 45 9 15 9 45 10 15 10 45 11 15 11 45 12 15 12 45 1 15 1 45 2 15 2 45 3 15 3 45 4 15 4 45 5 15 5 45 6 15 6 45 7 15 7 45 8 15 8 45 9 15
UNTHANK'S ROAD	8 45 ... 9 45 ... 10 45 ... 11 45 ... 12 45 ... 1 45 ... 2 45 ... 3 45 ... 4 45 ... 5 45 ... 6 45 ... 7 45 ... 8 45 ...
THORPE VILLAGE	... 9 30 ... 10 30 ... 11 30 ... 12 30 ... 1 30 ... 2 30 3 0 3 30 4 0 4 30 5 0 5 30 6 0 6 30 7 0 7 30 8 0 8 30 9 0 9 30
ROSARY CORNER	... 9 45 ... 10 45 ... 11 45 ... 12 45 ... 1 45 ... 2 45 3 15 3 45 4 15 4 45 5 15 5 45 6 15 6 45 7 15 7 45 8 15 8 45 9 15 9 45
BRACONDALE	... ... 10 15 ... 11 15 ... 12 15 ... 1 15 ... 2 15 ... 3 15 ... 4 15 ... 5 15 ... 6 15 ... 7 15 ... 8 15 . 9 15

TO	FROM THE MARKET PLACE.
ROSARY CORNER	9 0 ... 10 0 ... 11 0 ... 12 0 ... 1 0 ... 2 0 2 30 3 0 3 30 4 0 4 30 5 0 5 30 6 0 6 30 7 0 7 30 8 0 8 30 9 0 ...
THORPE VILLAGE	9 0 ... 10 0 ... 11 0 ... 12 0 ... 1 0 ... 2 0 2 30 3 0 3 30 4 0 4 30 5 0 5 30 6 0 6 30 7 0 7 30 8 0 8 30 9 0 ...
UNTHANK'S ROAD	... ... 10 30 ... 11 30 ... 12 30 ... 1 30 ... 2 30 ... 3 30 ... 4 30 ... 5 30 ... 6 30 ... 7 30 ... 8 30 ... ...
DEREHAM ROAD	9 0 9 30 10 0 10 30 11 0 11 30 12 0 12 30 1 0 1 30 2 0 2 30 3 0 3 30 4 0 4 30 5 0 5 30 6 0 6 30 7 0 7 30 8 0 8 30 9 0 9 30
N.CATTON { Pitt St.	8 30 9 30 ... 10 30 ... 11 30 ... 12 30 ... 1 30 ... 2 30 ... 3 30 ... 4 30 ... 5 30 ... 6 30 ... 7 30 ... 8 30 ...
{ Magst.	9 0 ... 10 0 ... 11 0 ... 12 0 ... 1 0 ... 2 0 ... 3 0 ... 4 0 ... 5 0 ... 6 0 ... 7 0 ... 8 0 ... 9 0 ...
NEWMARKET RD.	9 0 9 30 10 0 10 30 11 0 11 30 12 0 12 30 1 0 1 30 2 0 2 30 3 0 3 30 4 0 4 30 5 0 5 30 6 0 6 30 7 0 7 30 8 0 8 30 9 0 9 0
BRACONDALE	... 10 0 ... 11 0 ... 12 0 ... 1 0 ... 2 0 ... 3 0 ... 4 0 ... 5 0 ... 6 0 ... 7 0 ... 8 0 ... 9 0 ...

FARES—To or from the Market Place—Bracondale, Newmarket Road, New Catton, Dereham Road, Unthank's Road, Rosary Corner, 2d.; beyond Rosary Corner, 3d.

Children under 10 years of age, half-price. Babes in arms, free. No Smoking allowed, or Dogs admitted within the Company's Carriages. A covered and open Waggonette and an Omnibus are kept for Private Parties. Books of Tickets, for the convenience of Passengers, can be obtained at the Market Shelter, or of the Manager. By Order,

SAMUEL CULLEY,
Secretary.

From 28th May, 1883, until further Notice.

The buses were single-deckers with an inside seating capacity of 12 to 14 passengers. The driver's seat was high up, and alongside him was a seat which could accommodate an additional four or five passengers. Conductors were not employed and fares were collected by the driver through a trap door set in the roof of the bus. It is recorded that the buses were painted in gaudy colours, and it is known that green was used for vehicles on the Newmarket Road service and yellow for those on the Unthank Road and Earlham Road services.

Trace horses were used at certain places. The one on Guildhall Hill was a famous horse of the time called Jack, while the other, which assisted in pulling the bus up Thorpe Road past Thorpe station, does not appear to have been so famous. The buses that operated from Thorpe railway station to Thorpe Gardens were double-deckers with

117

Single-deck horse-drawn bus of the Norwich Omnibus Company.

knifeboard seating outside, and each bus was pulled by two horses. It may be that this service was operated by another company, but there is no known record.

The pioneers of the early tramways were a dauntless set of men, and it was a case of try and try again. At the end of the nineteenth century there were numerous inventors who were carrying out experiments with a view to the replacement of the horse as the principal form of tramway motive power, and one of these people was Andrew Hallidie, an American from San Francisco. His idea was, in brief, for a cable running in a conduit between the running rails to be attached to the car by a controllable gripper, the car getting its motion from the cable which was wound on and off a drum at the cable station. Hallidie proposed a scheme for Norwich and on 16th January, 1883, the Norwich Tramways Bill promoted by the Hallidie Patent Cable Tramways Corporation Limited was considered by the Parliamentary and By-Laws Committee of the Norwich City Council. The Committee, however, recommended that in consequence of the nuisance and discomfort which would have been caused by the construction and working of the proposed tramway, a petition be presented in Parliament against the Bill in its entirety. This report was adopted by the City Council and the company ultimately abandoned the scheme. (Hallidie's San Francisco cable tramway is still running, although more as a tourist attraction than as an important unit of the city's transport system.)

Incidentally, it is worth noting that the City Council did not come up with a scheme of tramways on its own behalf and appeared to prefer private companies to take the initiative in introducing schemes.

Three years after the Hallidie scheme, a further company known as the Norwich Tramways Company Limited, with offices in London and a capital of £30,000, was registered on 23rd December, 1886. The proposals of this company were agreed to by the City Council, and a Norwich Tramways Order was made in 1887 authorising the company to proceed with its scheme. On 17th December, 1889, it was reported to the Norwich City Council that notice had been received from the company that they intended to abandon the scheme of tramways authorised to them under the 1887 Order.

No further developments came for nine years, when two proposed schemes were submitted to the Council in the same year, 1896. The first was put in by the British Electric Traction Company, who were proposing to form a company to be known as the Norwich and District Light Railways to construct and work a network of light railways in the district with a view to bringing into closer connection the districts of Costessey, Thorpe St. Andrew, Trowse-Newton, Eaton, Beccles, Bungay and Hingham.

At the same time, the New General Traction Company Limited proposed to promote a Bill to incorporate a company, the Norwich Electric Tramways Company, to construct and work a network of tramways in the city of Norwich. In February, 1897, a petition by 23,500 inhabitants of the city in favour of the New General Traction Company Limited's scheme was presented to the City Council, which gave its consent to the Bill then before Parliament. The British Electric Traction Company had agreed to withdraw its proposals if they met with opposition from the City Council.

As a result the New General Traction Company Limited's Bill went through Parliament on 20th July, 1897, and in February, 1898, with 50 per cent of its capital of £240,000 having been paid-up, the Norwich Electric Tramways Company was authorised by the City Council to commence constructing the tramways. The New General Traction Company (formed in 1896) was a promoting company and, besides owning the Norwich Electric Tramways Company, owned from the start the bulk of the share capital of the Norwich and Coventry tramway companies and the Douglas Head Marine Drive tramways. Also owned by the New General Traction Company were the Light Railway Syndicate Limited, which obtained powers to build a 22-mile Central Essex Light Railway and a line in the U.S.A.

The City Council and the company negotiated the terms of the Council's agreement to the proposed tramways, and in so doing there was some hard bargaining over the responsibility for paying for the necessary road works entailed to enable the rails to be laid in Norwich's narrow streets. It was finally agreed that the cost of widening old streets and cutting a new street on St. Andrew's Hill through the buildings in Redwell Street, and demolishing Mr. Clarke's ironmongery shop on Orford Hill to enable the tramways to be laid from Castle Meadow into Red Lion Street, was to be equally shared between the company and the Council; the cost, incidentally, was £45,000. The final result was that two new streets were constructed, seven others widened, and other improvements carried out; the street alterations cost £100,000, of which the Corporation paid £66,000 and the company £34,000. In addition to the usual obligation to repair the tramway and the roadway between the rails and 18 inches on each side of the rails (Tramways Act, 1870), the company had to undertake (under the Norwich Tramways Act, 1897):

(a) To repair the whole road in the case of certain very narrow streets—the yardstick was whether the rails were laid within three feet of the kerb.
(b) To maintain the junction of the tramway paving with the road surface laid by the Council.

The initial Act provided for the laying of 5.3 miles of double track and 11.2 miles single track, but before construction commenced a further Act in 1898 added an additional 0.17 miles of double track and 0.83 miles single track to the original scheme, with a consequent increase in share capital of £24,000. There was also a clause in the Act which gave the City Council powers of compulsory purchase of the tramways after a period of 35 years.

On 22nd June, 1898, the work of constructing the tramways began. The first section was on the Thorpe Road and Earlham Road routes. The numerous curves made the construction no easy task, and the difficulty was further increased by the number of steep gradients which occurred on the curved sections. The narrowest street on the tramways was Theatre Street which was only 12 ft. 5 in. wide ; sharp curves were very numerous, and the radius of the sharpest (the junction of Red Lion Street and Rampant Horse Street) was 35 ft. The steepest gradient was 1 in 14.5.

The contract for the construction of the tramways was awarded to Pauling and Company Limited, of Westminster, London. The construction of the permanent way was of an unusual kind, at least for Britain, in that the rails were continuously welded. A comparatively light rail weighing 65.5 lb. per yard was used, except that on the curves rails of shorter length weighing 90 lb. per yard were used. In the case of the 65 lb. rails, the dimensions were: length 45 ft., depth 6 in., width of base 4½ in., width of head 3 in., width of groove 1 in., depth of groove 1⅛ in. The rails were clipped to sleepers laid at intervals of 5 ft., with tie-rods at 5 ft. intervals, as a result of which the track gauge of 3 ft. 6 in. was held to gauge at intervals of 2 ft. 6 in.

For the special trackwork Askham Bros. and Wilson's patent spring-operated points were used in some places, while for the other junctions movable and open points of crucible cast steel were supplied by the same manufacturers. The rails were embedded in the roadbed, which was formed of concrete on which there was a layer of sand, and on this were laid granite paving setts measuring 5 in. by 6 in. by 4 in. On certain sections wooden blocks were used in place of the granite setts.

The cast welding was perhaps the most interesting aspect, because the continuous rail joints in place of the ordinary joints did away with the evils of the latter type of joints; the actual welding of the rail joints was done by R. W. Blackwell and Company using the Falk process. The rail ends were thoroughly cleaned by a sand blast or emery wheel and then placed firmly together. A cast iron mould was

The Falk welding mould in position for track welding operations in Norwich.

then placed around the joint and molten iron of a special chemical composition was run into the mould. The molten iron used was heated to a much higher temperature than its fusing point, so that it heated up the rail to a white heat. When the metal had cooled, the casing was removed and, due to the cooling process, a very tight joint resulted. Any unevenness on the upper surface was ground down so that an ideally smooth track surface was obtained. Unfortunately, the cost was very high and, as a result, only a few undertakings adopted this type of continuous rail joint. The only bonds used were cross bonds at intervals of 200 yards.

The overhead trolley line, which was supplied by John A. Roebling's Sons Company of Trenton, New Jersey, U.S.A., was suspended by various means—centre poles with double brackets, side poles with single brackets, side poles with span wires, and wall rosettes to which span wires were attached (rosettes were a form of attachment fastened into the walls of buildings)—the actual choice depended upon the section of route. In certain places it was necessary to fit guard wires above the overhead trolley lines to protect them against other wires suspended above them, and a further interesting feature was the use in a number of cases of bracket arms which were slotted at the outer end, the hanger and insulator being fitted into the slot rather than hung from the arm. The trolley wire was composed of hard drawn copper, 98 per cent pure, of 0.32 in. diameter, and suspended in half-mile lengths. Steel poles were used and the brackets of iron were to a pattern specially designed by I. E. Winslow, the Chief Engineer of the New General Traction Company. On certain sections of the tramways, the centre poles were used to support two incandescent lamps.

By 1900, the tramways in Thorpe Road, Earlham Road, Magdalen Road, Riverside Road, Newmarket Road and Orford Place loop (known as the Tramway Centre) were constructed and trial trips were made over the completed sections on 19th April, 1900. At about this time the proposed services were made public. The Norwich Omnibus Company, which had ceased horse bus operation on 17th December, 1899, was wound up in May, 1900.

On 19th June, 1900, the overhead line equipment was inspected by A. P. Trotter, electrical inspector to the Board of Trade, and then on 26th July, 1900, Colonel Yorke, R.E., railways inspector to the Board of Trade, inspected the permanent way and cars. Colonel Yorke made one or two comments with regard to the centre poles in Prince of Wales Road (incidentally, there were four centre poles near the Haymarket in the Walk). He wanted these to be replaced by side poles and span wires. He also fixed stops, known as "Board of Trade stops,"

122

Orford Place, looking towards Castle Meadow, in early days. This illustration shows Brush-built cars in their original state.

A 1904 photograph of No. 2. Note the seat covers, destination boards, absence of electric headlamps, and the uniforms of the staff.

at which cars had to come to a compulsory halt. These were sited on gradients and, generally, at main traffic junctions. Otherwise all was in order and on 30th July, 1900, car No. 20 formally opened the tramways by traversing the routes on which services were commenced the same day. Fifty cars were available for the opening of the tramways, motor cars Nos. 1 to 40 and trailer cars Nos. 41 to 50. The routes opened were on Magdalen Road, Earlham Road, Dereham Road and Thorpe Road; Aylsham Road was opened on 1st August, 1900, Riverside Road and on to Mousehold on 5th August, 1900, and Newmarket Road on 10th August, 1900. The connecting tramway from the Royal Hotel to Bracondale and Trowse, via King Street, was opened on 5th September, 1900. It should be noted that the tramways were passed by the Board of Trade inspectors as a whole and were opened as and when sufficient staff became available.

In October, the local clergy sent a petition to the City Council protesting against Sunday services on the tramways, but the Town Clerk replied to the effect that the City Council had no power to order the Norwich Electric Tramways Company not to operate Sunday services and that the clergy should write to the Tramways Manager. This they did, but the Tramways Manager could not see his way clear to agree with their suggestion. On 13th December, 1900, the Unthank Road route was opened to traffic.

Staff recruited for the opening of the tramways had to purchase their own uniforms, and wages were 3d. per hour for a conductor and 4d. per hour for a motorman. No guaranteed week was in operation and there were no holidays. Other uniformed staff were a Chief Inspector and four Divisional Inspectors. Staff were issued with a rule book which had to be carried by all members of the staff when on duty. It was a slim booklet, bound in black leather with gold lettering, and incorporated about 75 rules, divided into three sections: rules for all, rules for conductors and rules for motormen. The rules stated specifically that the conductor was in charge of the car, having regard to the motorman's responsibilities.

Among the more interesting rules were:

Any crew backing a car without reversing the trolley make themselves liable to be dismissed.

Cars not allowed to pass on Guildhall Hill, St. Stephen's Street, or between Surrey Street and the Post Office [*not the present G.P.O.—author*]. Not more than two cars allowed on Foundry Bridge at the same time.

On approaching an overhead frog, Motorman will warn Conductor by single stroke of the foot gong. The Conductor must immediately take hold of trolley cord and retain same until trolley wheel has passed frog, and then give signal to go ahead promptly.

Dogs (except in the case of small dogs held in the lap) will not be allowed in the car.

Motormen must not be without their earth wire and spare main fuse when driving a car.

Cars must not approach nearer than thirty yards (about three car lengths) to a preceding car. This does not apply to Royal Hotel Junction, Orford Place, St. Giles Gates Junction or Redwell Street passing places.

Bell signals were:

"one" — stop
"two" — start
"three" — when moving—emergency stop
"three" — when stationary—back up.

Insofar as the direction of the company was concerned, there was a board of directors, one of whom was appointed by the City Council, but the day-to-day management was in the hands of the Tramways Manager, the first of whom was A. N. Bannister.

The tramways proved so successful that 400,000 passengers were carried in the first two weeks, but, unfortunately, due to the wheels being of "chilled iron of soft temper" there were a number of complaints of excessive noise. The wheels were progressively replaced and appropriate apologies were made by the company.

Connecting tramways were laid in Chapel Field Road, Chapel Field Road North, Magpie Road and Heigham Road. As a matter of interest, the only two places on the tramways where the cars could be turned around were at Orford Place and the junction of Bank Plain and Agricultural Hall Plain, where the rails formed a triangular arrangement. At the outset all services operated to and from Orford Place but, because of the acute congestion caused by some ten services converging on the Tramway Centre, where all cars had to reverse, this arrangement ceased at the end of March, 1901, when through cross-city services were introduced on most routes. There were certain exceptions and these are mentioned later in this chapter.

The company built its own two-storey brick power station in Duke Street, on the south side of the River Wensum. It was not erected without difficulty, as the boiler house and machine room had to be built on piles, due to the soft nature of the ground. One hundred piles from 28 ft. to 32 ft. long were used, and a concrete foundation was laid on them. To erect the chimney satisfactorily it was necessary to excavate the soft earth until the gravel was reached, and then lay a bed of concrete 25 ft. square and 25 ft. thick on this gravel; the chimney itself was built on the concrete base and was made of brick to a height of 120 ft.

In the lower room of the boiler house were four Babcock and Wilcox water tube boilers, each of 300 h.p. Each boiler had a heating surface of 3,240 square feet and was capable of supplying steam at a pressure of 160 lb. per square inch. Fuel was supplied to each boiler by means of a Bellis mechanical stoker and conveyor, which was driven by a 10 h.p. electric motor. Water for the boilers was taken from the River Wensum by means of Worthington pumps and 1 lb. of soda was added per 1,000 gallons. In an emergency there was an arrangement for taking water from the town supply. The fuel used was slack, and it was delivered in barges and unloaded into sheds alongside the power station.

The machinery room contained four generating sets. Messrs. Browett, Lindley and Company of Patricroft, Manchester, supplied four tandem horizontal engines, running at 200 revolutions per minute, and each capable of developing 400 to 500 h.p. with 150 lb. pressure. There were two flywheels, one on each side of the engine, and one of the wheels contained the governor which was of the Begtrup type, actuating the piston valve which controlled the admission of steam to the high-pressure cylinder. There were four dynamos of the Westinghouse engine type; they were coupled direct to the Browett-Lindley engines and when running at 200 revolutions per minute developed 200 kilowatts at 550 volts d.c. In addition to the large dynamos, there was a small plant for lighting the power station when the large machines were not in use. This small plant consisted of a Westinghouse vertical steam engine, directly coupled to a small Westinghouse dynamo capable of developing 15 kilowatts at 500 volts when making 390 revolutions per minute.

The switchboard, of the Westinghouse railway panel type, was composed of white marble and had Weston ammeters and voltmeters and two Elliot Brothers' recording instruments. There were ten continuous panels, one Board of Trade panel, one panel for the 15-kilowatt generator, and two spare panels. The generators, the 10 h.p. motor for working the conveyors, and the switchboard, were supplied by the British Westinghouse Electric and Manufacturing Company. A travelling crane, running the whole length of the machinery room, and capable of lifting five tons, was supplied by Messrs. Jessop and Appleby.

Current at 550 volts d.c. was fed to the trolley line at various intervals of 440 to 880 yards. There were nine feeder cables laid in Doulton conduits; the feeders were supplied by the British Insulated Wire Company Limited of Prescot, Lancashire. These feeders were directed to switch boxes as follows:

No. 1 Feeder
To Barn Road box, and fed Dereham Road, Barn Road, Aylsham Road and Magpie Road.

No. 2 Feeder
To St. Giles Gate box, and fed St. Giles Junction and Unthank Road.

No. 3 Feeder
To St. Giles Gate box, and fed St. Giles to the Old Mortimers Hotel and Earlham Road.

No. 4 Feeder
To Orford Place box, from there to Coburg Street (St. Stephen's Gate box), and fed St. Stephen's Street, St. Stephen's Gate, Newmarket Road, Chapel Field Road and Queens Road.
The St. Stephen's Gate box was later modified in that the Chapel Field feeder was removed when the tramways were lifted.

No. 5 Feeder
To Orford Place box, from there to St. Stephen's Plain box, and fed St. Stephen's Street, Queens Road, City Road, Bracondale, Theatre Street, Chapel Field Road.

No. 6 Feeder
To Orford Place box, and fed Orford Place, Haymarket, Guildhall Hill and as far as Old Mortimers Hotel.

No. 7 Feeder
To Royal Hotel box, and fed Royal Hotel Junction and Castle Meadow.

No. 8 Feeder

To Royal Hotel box, and fed Magdalen Road and car sheds.

No. 9 Feeder

To Royal Hotel box, from there to Foundry Bridge, and fed Thorpe Road, Riverside Road and Prince of Wales Road. This feeder also went to St. James Hill box and fed Riverside Road and Mousehold Heath.

Each section was controlled from the switchboxes and could, if necessary, be isolated without affecting the remaining sections controlled by the particular box.

The car sheds and repair shops were situated at Silver Road. There were two sheds, one 90 ft. by 60 ft. and the other 106 ft. by 60 ft. There were six tracks in each shed with accommodation for 50 cars. In one shed there were three inspection pits and in the other shed two such pits. The repair shop was 60 ft. by 61 ft. and contained drilling machines, wheel lathes, travelling crane, and a car wheel grinder supplied by the Hampden Carborundum Wheel Company of Springfield, Massachusetts, U.S.A. The grinder was driven by an electric motor, and the emery wheel made 1,500 revolutions per minute, while the car wheel made 13 revolutions per minute. The emery dust was collected by means of a small centrifugal fan. When the wheel grinder was not in use, it could be lowered beneath the level of the floor, leaving the track free. The body repair and the paint shops were also situated at Silver Road. In addition to the above, there was also a forge. The offices were situated on Timber Hill, with the main office of the General Manager, his staff and clerks, near the Bell Hotel, and the parcels office opposite.

The total cost of the undertaking was £300,000.

When it was decided generally to abandon the practice of turning cars at Orford Place, and after all the extensions were opened, the following services were operated:

Unthank Road (Jenny Lind Hospital)—Orford Place—Magdalen Road—Silver Road
White destination indicator board.
Through running time 35 minutes.
Cars operated at intervals of eleven minutes (winter), eight minutes (summer).

No. 29 in St. Giles Street, Norwich.   *Photo: Courtesy J. H. Price*

No. 32 in Unthank Road, Norwich. This car was subsequently transferred to Coventry.   *Photo: Courtesy J. H. Price*

I

An early photograph of Nos. 40 and 16 at the Royal Hotel end of Castle Meadow. No. 16 was subsequently transferred to Coventry.

Photo: Courtesy W. E. Deamer

Car No. 31 in Prince of Wales Road.   *Photo: Courtesy J. H. Price*

Thorpe Road (Redan)—Thorpe Railway Station—Orford Place—Newmarket Road (Eaton Hill).
Green destination indicator board.
Through running time 33 minutes.
Cars operated at intervals of eleven minutes (winter), eight minutes (summer).

Gurney Road (Bandstand) summer, *or Nelson Barracks (Riverside Road)* winter—*Orford Place—Earlham Road (Cemetery Gates).*
Red destination indicator board.
Through running time:
    (a) Bandstand—Cemetery, 35 minutes.
    (b) Nelson Barracks—Cemetery, 25 minutes.
Cars operated at intervals of eleven minutes (winter), ten minutes (summer); after 10.40 a.m. (summer) extended to the Bandstand (Mousehold).

Dereham Road (Merton Road)—Orford Place; operated alternately *via St. Andrews Street or Heigham Street and St. Giles.*
Blue destination indicator board.
Through running time 18 minutes.
Cars operated at intervals of eleven minutes (winter), nine minutes (summer).

City Road (top of Long John Hill)—Orford Place—King Street—Trowse railway station.
Green/red destination indicator board.
Cars operated at intervals of 15 minutes (winter and summer).

Aylsham Road (Vicarage Road)—City Station—St. Andrews Street—Thorpe Railway Station.
Blue/red destination indicator board.
Through running time 22 minutes.
Cars operated at intervals of 12 minutes (winter and summer).
When this service commenced and operated between Aylsham Road and Orford Place, cars operated alternately via City Station and Barn Road, and via Magdalen Road and Magpie Road.

Services on all routes started between 6.30 a.m. and 7 a.m. on weekdays, and 10 and 10.30 a.m. on Sundays. There was, however, some reduction in the frequencies at which the services operated during the early morning and late evening. Last cars left Orford Place at approximately 11 p.m., depending on the particular service concerned. Due to the presence of carts which served the market, obstructing the

131

westbound track in the Walk, cars proceeding towards Unthank Road and Earlham Road before 9 a.m. were routed via Theatre Street and Chapel Field North along which a special tramway was laid for this purpose.

Waybills were made up by conductors at each terminus and at Orford Place. In early days a system was introduced of numbering overhead line poles to coincide with numerical ticket stages.

At the opening of the tramways in 1900 the fares were set as follows (per Norwich Electric Tramways Company official fare tables):

"The Circle referred to herein takes its centre at Orford Place and extends to the following points: Thorpe Station; Crown Brewery; King Street; Ber Street Gates; City Road; Fountain; Newmarket Road; St. Giles Gates; St. Benedict's Gate; St. Clement's Church, Magdalen Street.
FARE, from any one point to any other point within the Circle, 1d.

Between	and	Fare
Terminus — City Road		
„ — Unthank Road		
„ — Dereham Road		
„ — Aylsham Road	Orford Place	1d.
„ — Magdalen Road		
„ — Thorpe Road		
„ — Trowse Station		

From above places to any point within the Circle beyond Orford Place, 1d.

„ any other terminus to any other terminus, except 'Eaton' or 'Mousehold Heath'	
„ Christchurch Road to terminus of any route	
„ Cavalry Barracks to terminus of any route	
„ Eaton to Orford Place	2d.
„ Mousehold Heath to Orford Place	
„ Eaton to any point within the Circle beyond Orford Place	
„ Mousehold Heath to any point within the Circle beyond Orford Place	2½d.
„ Eaton to terminus of any other route	
„ Mousehold Heath to terminus of any other route	3d.

132

Passengers wishing to travel over more than one route are required to ask for a 'Transfer Ticket' when paying their fare, as transfer will not be given after the fare has been collected.

Passenger parcels
For one article, if larger than a small handbag, 1d.

Unaccompanied parcels
For parcels not exceeding 14 lb., 24 in. in length, 15 in. in width, 10 in. in depth—charge for any distance, 1d.

Workmen's tickets
Return fares for artisans, mechanics and daily labourers travelling during the hours specified under the statutory powers, shall be charged at a price not exceeding the single fares charged to ordinary passengers travelling the single journey with a minimum fare of 2d.

1st November to 28th February
Twelve journeys for 6d. available up to 8.30 a.m., and 4.30 p.m. to 7.15 p.m. Not available on Sundays, holidays, or after 2 p.m. on Saturdays.

1st March to 31st October
Twelve journeys for 6d. available up to 8.30 a.m., between 12 noon to 2.30 p.m., and 5 p.m. to 7.15 p.m. Not available on Sundays, holidays or after 2 p.m. on Saturdays.

Schoolchildren's tickets
Twelve journeys for 6d. available 8.30 a.m. to 9.30 a.m., 12 noon to 12.30 p.m., 1 p.m. to 1.30 p.m., 4.30 p.m. to 5.30 p.m. Not available on Saturday, Sundays or Bank Holidays."

A rather unusual ticket-issuing system was in use on the Norwich Electric Tramways Company (a similar system was in use on the Coventry Electric Tramways Company, another of the New General Traction Company subsidiary companies). The method was that the conductor had a cylindrical canister with a spool on to which he slid rolls of tickets, each roll separated by a circular piece of cardboard. The tickets projected through a slot at the face side of the canister and were torn off as required; to punch (and therefore cancel the ticket) the conductor had a hand punch which registered the number of tickets issued.

An original Brush-bodied car at Trowse. Note the conductor's ticket-issuing canister.

As the canister could only be opened at one end, it follows that the tickets least used were inserted to project at the closed end of the canister, and those most used at the opening end of the canister. Tickets were issued in bulk to conductors in the following quantities— 2,000 at 1d., 1½d. and 2d.; 1,000 at 2½d.; 400 at 3d. and 3½d. These were all roll tickets; only scholars', parcels and workpeople's tickets were made up in packs.

As conductors required fresh stocks, they indented for them to the ticket office, which was situated near the Bell Hotel on Timber Hill. Tickets were serially numbered.

The original tickets had the names of the fare stages printed on them, but this later gave way to stage numbers. In later years, when fares of higher value were charged, tickets were "married"; that is, two tickets were issued to one passenger to make up the fare. The canister and roll ticket system was in use on the trams, and later the buses, until the Norwich Omnibus Company was formed.

To indicate to the public the car's destination, narrow side route boards and small destination boxes were used, but by 1904 coloured route boards were introduced with the main roads traversed clearly indicated. At a later date these were further supplemented by larger route boards which were displayed along the waist rail of the car and

134

almost extended from corner pillar to corner pillar. Eventually, these boards were abbreviated (by 1920) to the length of the two central window pillars. A coloured "bull's eye" light for use during hours of darkness corresponded with the colour of the boards.

One of the most interesting operating features was that the Norwich Electric Tramways Company took the somewhat unusual step of introducing trailer cars—nicknamed "Matchboxes." These were similar in appearance to, but smaller than, the motor cars, and were used on the service to Trowse and for such purposes as outings. The main Board of Trade regulations relating to the operation of trailer cars on the Norwich Electric Tramways Company were as follows:

(a) When two cars were running together, it was necessary for there to be a brakesman on the front platform of the second car (in addition to the conductor), whose sole duty was to attend to the brake. Means had to be provided for the driver to signal to this man when he wished the brake on the rear car to be applied.

(b) The cars had to be connected by double couplings, one of which had to be a rigid or close coupling.

As it was apparently necessary to employ four men to work the coupled motor and trailer cars, the economics of the arrangement might seem obscure, bearing in mind that this arrangement resulted in a smaller seating capacity for the same crew cost than did the operating of two motor cars. However, it is suggested that the looked-for benefits of this multiple-unit operation were expected from the greater seating capacity which could be offered over the single-track sections, thereby saving in the cost of constructing double-track tramways which, perhaps, only required a heavy service at irregular intervals.

Some difficulty was experienced with traffic congestion at Orford Place, due to the limited trackwork, and in 1904 the track was relaid with a view to easing the position. In the same year the section in the Norwich Tramways Act, 1897, regarding the company's responsibility for maintaining the roadway at the junction of the setts and the macadam, resulted in the City Council summoning the Norwich Electric Tramways Company for road repairs. In 1906 the Court decided in favour of the City Council and the company had to repair all the potholes just outside the setts over 13½ route miles.

During 1907, one of the City Aldermen—Alderman Green—when travelling on one of the cars, dropped his ticket on the floor of the car

135

while getting up to give his seat to a lady passenger. A ticket-checking inspector asked Alderman Green for his ticket, which he could not produce, and at the same time he declined to "scratch about" for the ticket or purchase another ticket. The company successfully prosecuted Alderman Green, and this incident—coupled with the legal case over the road repairs—did not assist in fostering good relations between the company and the City Council.

In 1909 Bannister resigned, to be succeeded by Ketley who was succeeded in 1919 by Foster, who was manager until Jewell was appointed a year later. Under Ketley's management, relations between the company and the City Council soon improved.

It is believed that during these earlier years some members of the staff of the Norwich and Coventry undertakings used to be attached to the Douglas Southern each summer. Ketley had been manager of the Douglas Head Marine Drive tramway until his appointment to the Norwich undertaking.

On the occasion of the visit to Norwich of King Edward VII in 1909, the Norwich Electric Tramways Company, besides catering for the very heavy traffic, had its cars drawn up at vantage points and used as grandstands ; charges were 1s. on top and 6d. inside.

It is perhaps noteworthy that King Street, one of the narrower streets of Norwich, carried double tramway track with numerous crossovers, although it did not have a frequent ordinary tram service. This, it is suggested, can only be accounted for by its use in early days for storage purposes on the occasion of a royal visit, such as is mentioned above, or of events at Crown Point (where, for instance, the Royal Show took place in 1911), at Carrow Abbey, home of the Colman family, and perhaps cross-city workpeople's services for the benefit of persons employed at Colman's factory.

A service which was introduced in 1910, but which lasted for only a short time, was from Heigham Road, via Chapel Field, to City Road (yellow destination board). This service, which had replaced a service from Dereham Road to Orford Place, via Heigham Road, was itself replaced in 1910 by a service from City Road to Orford Place (yellow/red destination board). The service from Trowse then operated via King Street to the G.P.O.; this severed the link between Trowse and Orford Place. As a result of these changes, the tramways in Heigham Road and Chapel Field Road fell into disuse as far as service cars were concerned. A further alteration made in 1910 was the linking of the Aylsham Road service with the Trowse service, thereby providing a through service via King Street to Trowse; the Royal Hotel to Thorpe Station section of the Aylsham Road service was therefore discontinued.

These changes may be summarised as follows:

Services in operation, 1911

Service	Destination board
Earlham Road (Cemetery Gates)—Nelson Barracks and Mousehold Bandstand (summer)	Red
Unthank Road (Jenny Lind Hospital)—Silver Road depôt	Opal white
Aylsham Road—Trowse Railway Station	Blue/Red
Newmarket Road (Eaton Hill)—Thorpe Road (Redan)	Green
City Road (top of Long John Hill)—Orford Place	Yellow/Red
Dereham Road (Merton Road)—Orford Place	Blue

In 1911 it was apparent that the trailer car experiment was not a success, and of the ten trailers five were scrapped and five (Nos. 43–47) were motorised and put to work on the service from Aylsham Road to Trowse. At the same time, experience of operating the services on the tramways had indicated a lack of sufficient passing loops, and as a result new loops were laid in Dereham Road.

For a short time a service was operated from Unthank Road to Thorpe Road and another from Earlham Road to Magdalen Road (Silver Road depôt), but when the Unthank Road to Magdalen Road service was resumed, through tickets were issued to Aylsham Road, a car on the service to Aylsham Road operating via Magpie Road to Magdalen Gates, where a connection was made with the Unthank Road–Magdalen Road cars. This facility was later discontinued.

To meet the demand for additional and extended services created by new housing on the outskirts of the city, the company proposed a number of new tramways:

Tramways proposed	Track mileage (in furlongs and chains)		
	Single	Double	Total
1. St. Andrews Road/Duke Street, via Duke Street, to link with the Aylsham Road tramway	——	4 fur. 2.6 ch.	4 fur. 2.6 ch.

2. Via Timber Hill, Ber Street to Bracondale	2 fur. 1.9 ch.	2 fur. 1.6 ch	4 fur. 3.5 ch.
3. From Queens Road/City Road junction to the Bracondale/King Street junction, thus linking Queens Road and Trowse via Bracondale	2 fur. 6.7 ch.	3.0 ch.	2 fur. 9.7 ch.
4. From Unthank Road terminus, via Unthank Road to Judges Walk	2 fur. 9.15 ch.	3.0 ch.	3 fur. 2.15 ch.
5. From Denmark Road terminus along Sprowston Road to Mousehold Lane	4 fur. 4.85 ch.	3.0 ch.	4 fur. 7.85 ch.
6. From Thorpe Road terminus along Thorpe Road to Thorpe Village	2 fur. 9.0 ch.	6.0 ch.	3 fur. 9.0 ch.
7, 8, 9 and 10. Relaying of the Unthank Road, Earlham Road junction.	⸺	⸺	⸺

On 31st July, 1914, the Norwich Electric Tramways Company obtained powers to construct tramways 3 to 10 inclusive. The same Act authorised the company to abandon the tramway in King Street from the Prince of Wales Road/King Street junction to the King Street/Bracondale junction and, perhaps more important in the light of later events, to operate buses when the running of trams was "impracticable or during construction, alteration or repair of the tramway route, the extension of which may be contemplated by the company."

Other tramway extensions considered at the time but not proceeded with were the abandonment of the tramways in St. Stephen's Street, Queen's Road and Hall Road, and the substitution of a service to the Lakenham district straight from the Tramways Centre, via Ber Street or Surrey Street, to Bracondale. Extension tramways were proposed along Earlham Road and Newmarket Road, but if the St. Stephen's link had been discontinued, how the Newmarket Road service was to be operated was not explained. But then these proposals were only tentative and not in final form.

By this time wages had risen to 3¼d. per hour for conductors and 4½d. per hour for motormen.

In pursuance of the proposal to operate buses under the conditions mentioned above, the company purchased two A.E.C. vehicles and these were in process of being delivered when war broke out in 1914. As a result, the vehicles, which had reached Ipswich, were commandeered by the military authorities. However, in 1915, the company introduced a bus service from Thorpe tram terminus to St. Andrew's Hospital (Thorpe War Hospital). The single fare was 2d. but, owing to objections from the Great Eastern Railway, the service was discontinued at the end of the war in 1918.

Of course, the 1914–18 war put a stop to the schemes mentioned above, and the company faced many difficulties of shortage of metals, coal for power, and manpower. Motormen, conductors and skilled fitters were recruited into the armed forces, and conductresses (but no women motormen—or should it be motorwomen!) were employed. As a result of all these shortages, the services were curtailed, late journeys were deleted from the time-tables, and the Sunday services commenced at 2.15 p.m. In 1917 cars were fitted with notices which could be displayed to warn the public of an impending air-raid. These notices read—"Hostile Aircraft Approaching—Take Cover."

Towards the end of the First World War an aerodrome and armaments works were established on the northern fringe of Mousehold Heath, which is situated on the north-eastern perimeter of the city. As the site was remote from the railway, it was necessary to find some alternative means of transport for the raw materials and finished products, so to meet this requirement the War Department approached the Norwich Electric Tramways Company, as it was thought that they might be able to assist. At this time the service via King Street to Trowse Station was much reduced and, as mentioned, the company had obtained powers under the 1914 Act to abandon the tramway in King Street. Accordingly, at the request of the War Department, the company agreed to construct a light railway to the works, but steel rails, copper and other materials necessary for the construction of the permanent way and overhead trolley line were virtually unobtainable, so it was decided to abandon the King Street tramway and use the rails and other equipment to construct the light railway.

On 28th April, 1918, the service between Aylsham Road and Trowse was cut back to the Royal Hotel and, insofar as street transport was concerned, Trowse became isolated as the link along Bracondale was not constructed for eighteen months. The rails in King Street were lifted, the overhead dismantled, and used in the construction of the Mousehold Light Railway. This light railway was an extension of the

139

A view of the tram route on Mousehold Heath—obviously a popular resort on a fine day!

existing street tramway which terminated near the Bandstand (on Mousehold Heath) from where the line crossed the Heath in a shallow cutting roughly parallel to Gurney Road. The rails were spiked to 5 ft.-long wooden sleepers which were lightly laid in the soil of the Heath; the track was single, and at the far side of the Heath it crossed Mousehold Lane and continued into the factory premises. At this point there was a loop from which several sidings radiated, but as the overhead trolley line terminated at the loop, a small steam locomotive was used for motive power in the works area. This locomotive had the axle and frames altered, to suit the 3 ft. 6 in. gauge, by employees of the Norwich Electric Tramways Company. From the Bandstand to the works is a distance of 0.6 of a mile.

The light railway was constructed in a few weeks, presumably under the Defence of the Realm Regulations in place of the usual Light Railway Order, which would have been necessary for a line such as the one concerned.

Two specially built "powered wagons" (see schedule of cars) each hauled one or two flat cars and were driven by crews trained from among sixteen volunteers, who were paid a special bonus of 5s. per week. Apparently the "powered wagons" were kept at the works as

140

the crews detailed to work them started at 7 a.m. and travelled to the aerodrome in one of the motorised trailer cars (Nos. 43–47); the car was parked on the loop until the crew came off duty between 5 p.m. and 6 p.m., when they returned to the depôt with the car they had taken up. In all probability workpeople were conveyed on these workings.

During the day, one or both of the "powered wagons" would work between the aerodrome and Thorpe railway station, from where a single track spur was laid to Riverside Road. In the station forecourt, between Riverside Road and the end of the spur, there was a loop with spring-loaded points; this spur was used to enable the "powered wagons" to run round the trailers. At the station end of the spur there was a fork along what was platform 6 (now platform 5) by the ramp, but about three feet higher, for the purpose of transhipping materials between the light railway and railway wagons.

The light railway was regularly in use until the cessation of hostilities in November, 1918, and besides the shipment of raw materials, aircraft spares were also conveyed. After the war the "powered wagons" were handed over to the Norwich Electric Tramways Company, who used the mechanical units to build new cars with bodies supplied by the English Electric Company. The overhead line equipment between the Bandstand and the aerodrome was dismantled and the rails were lifted in the late 1930s, when tramway operation ceased on the main system; the rails in the works area were lifted when the premises were taken over by local light engineering firms. In 1957 the last remaining feature of the light railway was removed when the spur in Thorpe station forecourt was covered over as a result of the yard being resurfaced. The locomotive remained derelict for several years, but was eventually sold to Chessington Zoo.

In 1919, in accordance with the powers authorised under the 1914 Act, the Norwich Electric Tramways Company laid the connecting tramway between City Road and King Street, via Bracondale. The service between Orford Place and Trowse, but now via Queen's Road and Bracondale, was restored in the autumn of 1919; cars operating on the Orford Place to Trowse service carried an orange destination board; a second car on the Orford Place to City Road service gave a half-hourly service to each terminus with a quarter-hourly service from the top of Bracondale to the city.

As the men were released from the armed forces, the services on the tramways were gradually resurrected, Sunday services commencing at

141

11.30 a.m. In twelve months the services were back to normal. At about the same time, the tramways in Chapel Field Road, from its junction with Chapel Field North and St. Stephen's Gate, were abandoned. These tramways had been used by cars operating on the service from Heigham Road to City Road, this service having been discontinued (see above).

In 1920, as a result of these modifications, the track mileage was 19 miles, 2 furlongs, and 100 yards, and the services operated were as follows:

Service	Destination board	Service frequency (minutes)
Unthank Road—Magdalen Road	Opal white	6–7½
Thorpe Road—Earlham Road	Red	7½–10
Newmarket Road—Riverside Road (Mousehold Bandstand in summer)	Green	10–12
Dereham Road—Royal Hotel	Blue	7½–10
Aylsham Road—Royal Hotel	Red/Blue	15–30
City Road—Orford Place	Red/Yellow	30
Trowse Station—Orford Place	Orange	30
Thorpe Station—Orford Place (peak hours and Saturdays)	Green/White	no set frequency
Heigham Road—Orford Place via St. Andrew's (Saturdays)	Red/White	

To facilitate operating efficiency on single-track sections, automatic colour light signals were installed as follows:

(a) *Unthank Road and Magdalen Road*
Lights at Mount Pleasant, Cambridge Street (two-way), Park Lane, Tombland, St. Clement's Church, Magdalen Gates, Albany Road, Catton Church and Sprowston Road.

(b) *Dereham Road and Royal Hotel*
Lights at Exchange Street and Bank Plain.

As a result of increased costs, the company was getting into financial difficulties and on 13th October, 1920, it was granted an Order under the Tramways (Temporary Increases in Charges) Act, 1920, which provided that if it appeared to the Minister of Transport that there was ground for making an Order under the Act, and that if the case was one of urgency, he could make an Interim Order increasing the statutory maximum charges by such amount, not exceeding 100 per cent and subject to such conditions as he thought proper.

This Order (in respect of the Norwich Electric Tramways Company) provided that:

(a) The company should appoint stages not less than half a mile in length, and should not charge any fare for the conveyance of ordinary passengers in excess of the following:

> 2 stages 1½d.
> 3 stages 2d.
> 4 stages 2½d. Each stage to commence and terminate as nearly
> 5 stages 3d. as possible at a recognised traffic point.
> 6 stages 3½d.

(b) That return tickets for workmen should be issued at fares not exceeding the single fares presented by the Order for ordinary passengers travelling the single journey, based on 2d. and 2½d. (In practice this was a ½d. "blanket" increase on all fares.)

It was necessary to renew the Order every six months and this was done at intervals until operation ceased on the tramways.

Automatic points were in operation at Foundry Bridge and at St. Giles' Gate, but in general points were changed by the motorman with a point bar carried on the car. On single-track sections, passing loops had spring-loaded points operating in favour of the car entering the loop from the single-track section, cars leaving the loops forcing the points over by the car's momentum. At the complicated junction near the General Post Office in Prince of Wales Road, a point-boy was employed to change the points.

Other improvements carried out at this time were the doubling of the track onwards from Barn Road to Oak Street; laying in a double junction at the Royal Hotel and doubling the track in Upper King Street and Tombland; extending the double track in Unthank Road from Grosvenor Road to Park Lane Corner; doubling the remainder of St. Stephen's Street and continuing the double track along Red Lion Street to Orford Place: double junction at St. Giles' Gate (tramways 7, 8, 9, 10), and the introduction of additional passing loops on single-track sections.

During 1923 the first of the rebodied cars entered service (Nos. 7 and 9 using trucks and electrical equipment from ex-Mousehold Light

Railway "powered wagons") and were followed by a number of other similarly rebodied cars (see schedule of cars). The new bodies arrived by train at the City goods station, Alterations had to be made to the doors at the car sheds to enable the rebodied cars to enter without suffering damage to their canopies.

The 20 years' wear of continuous tramway traffic over the light rails, coupled with the difficulties of maintenance during the war years, began to take its toll and there was, unfortunately, not sufficient money available to spend on extensive renewals of the permanent way. This resulted in continual patching of the roadway adjacent to and between the rails. The City Council wanted to see an end of the setts, and the internal combustion engine had developed—mainly as a result of war necessity—to a stage not dreamed of 15 years previously. Some radical development in the company's policy was becoming necessary and it is not surprising to learn that in 1924 it decided to introduce motor buses on certain services.

It is interesting that the company introduced buses under the terms of the 1914 Act, without promoting a Bill to obtain an Act to abandon the tramways and substitute buses. The bus garage was established at the rear of the car sheds and was approached by way of Silver Road and Ladysmith Road.

On 19th April, 1925, the tramway from Aylsham Road via City Station was abandoned and, as a result, the service from Aylsham Road to the Royal Hotel ceased. In place of the tramway service, two bus services were introduced on 20th April, 1925:

Service 1—Duke Street, Pitt Street, St. Augustine's Gate, Aylsham Road, Mile Cross.
Service 2—St. Andrew's Plain, City Station, Oak Street, Drayton Road.

The services were operated by double-deck Guy vehicles.

In 1925, on 15th October, feeder bus services operated by one-man vehicles were introduced; these were:

Service (feeder) 4—Earlham tram terminus via Colman Road and Unthank Road (passing near Unthank Road tram terminus) to Judges Walk.

This service was later amended to operate from Earlham (tram

Norwich Electric Tramways Company.

Service between the City & Earlham Fiveways & Golf Links.

(Transfer Tram to Bus at Earlham Tram Terminus).

TIME TABLE COMING INTO OPERATION ON 1st DECEMBER, 1933.

Dep. Thorpe.	Dep. Orford Place.	Earlham Tram Terminus.	Arr. Earlham Fiveways.	Arr. Municipal Golf Links.	Dep. Golf Links.	Dep. Earlham Fiveways.	Arr. Earlham Tram Terminus	Arr. Orford Place.	Arr. Thorpe
A.M.	A.M.	A.M.	A.M.			A.M.	A.M.	A.M.	A.M.
		7.18	7.24			7.24	7.30	7.42	7.54
	7.18	7.30	7.36			7.36	7.42	7.54	8.6
	7.36	7.48	7.54			7.54	8.0	8.12	8.24
7.36	7.48	8.0	8.6			8.12	8.18	8.30	8.42
7.54	8.6	8.18	8.24			8.24	8.30	8.42	8.54
8.6	8.18	8.30	8.36			8.36	8.42	8.54	9.6
8.24	8.36	8.48	8.54			8.54	9.0	9.12	9.24
8.36	8.48	9.0	9.6			9.12	9.18	9.30	9.42
8.54	9.6	9.18	9.24			9.24	9.30	9.42	9.54
9.6	9.18	9.30	9.36			9.36	9.42	9.54	10.6
9.24	9.36	9.48	9.54			9.54	10.0	10.12	10.24
9.36	9.48	10.0	10.6			10.12	10.18	10.30	10.42
9.54	10.6	10.18	10.24			10.24	10.30	10.42	10.54
10.6	10.18	10.30	10.36			10.36	10.42	10.54	11.6
10.24	10.36	10.48	10.54			10.54	11.0	11.12	11.24
*10.36	*10.48	*11.0	*11.6			*11.12	*11.18	*11.30	*11.42
10.54	11.6	11.18	11.24			11.24	11.30	11.42	11.54
11.6	11.18	11.30	11.36			11.36	11.42	11.54	12.6 p.m.
11.24	11.36	11.48	11.54			11.54	12.0	12.12 p.m.	12.24
11.36	11.48	12.0	12.6 p.m			12.12 p.m.	12.18 p.m.	12.30	*12.42
11.54	12.6 p.m	12.18 p.m	12.24			12.24	12.30	12.42	12.54
12.6 p.m.	12.18	12.30	12.36			12.36	12.42	12.54	1.6
12.24	12.36	12.48	12.54			12.54	1.0	1.12	1.24
12.36	12.48	1.0	1.6	1.8	1.10	1.12	1.18	1.30	1.42
12.54	1.6	1.18	1.24			1.24	1.30	1.42	1.54
1.6	1.18	1.30	1.36			1.36	1.42	1.54	2.6
1.24	1.36	1.48	1.54			1.54	2.0	2.12	2.24
1.36	1.48	2.0	2.6	2.8	2.10	2.12	2.18	2.30	2.42
1.54	2.6	2.18	2.24			2.24	2.30	2.42	2.54
2.6	2.18	2.30	2.36			2.36	2.42	2.54	3.6
2.24	2.36	2.48	2.54			2.54	3.0	3.12	3.24
2.36	2.48	3.0	3.6	3.8	3.10	3.12	3.18	3.30	3.42
2.54	3.6	3.18	3.24			3.24	3.30	3.42	3.54
3.6	3.18	3.30	3.36			3.36	3.42	3.54	4.6
3.24	3.36	3.48	3.54			3.54	4.0	4.12	4.24
3.36	3.48	4.0	4.6	4.8	4.10	4.12	4.18	4.30	4.42
			And repeat every hour until						
10.6	10.18	10.30	10.36			10.36	10.42	10.54	11.6
10.24	10.36	10.48	10.54			10.54	11.0	11.12	—
10.36	10.48	11.0	11.6			11.6	11.12	11.24	—

*Sunday Service Commences.

LAST BUSES FROM GOLF LINKS AS UNDER :

January, 5.10 p.m.; February & March, 6.10 p.m.; April, 8.10 p.m.; May, June & July, 10.10 p.m.; August, 9.10 p.m.; September, 8.10 p.m.; October, 6.10 p.m.; November, 5.10 p.m.; December, 4.10 p.m.

NOTE—On Saturdays there is a 5 Minutes' Tram Service on Earlham and Thorpe, therefore Buses will depart from Earlham Tram Terminus at the hours, 15, 30, and 45 minutes.

BUSES LEAVE GOLF LINKS at 8 Minutes past the hour SATURDAYS ONLY.

Bus Fares—Earlham Tram Terminus & Earlham Fiveways - **1d.**

  „ „ & Golf Links - **1½d.**

Transfer Tickets—Tram & Bus, Orford Place & Golf Links - **3d.**

terminus) via Colman Road to Jessop Road and eventually merged with service 17 when that service commenced (see below).

Service (feeder) 5—Earlham, tram terminus, to Earlham, Fiveways; certain journeys extended to Golf Links, service operated every 15 minutes.

(See timetable on previous page.)

By 1926 wage rates had risen to 11d. per hour for conductors and 1s. 1d. per hour for motormen, the working week had been fixed at 64 hours, and the company paid an allowance for uniforms. A man with ten years' service was entitled to one week's paid holiday.

The general office was moved in 1926 from Timber Hill to a building which had originally been built as a boot factory in 1907 and which adjoined the tramway depôt at Silver Road. In 1927, Castle Meadow was widened from being a narrow thoroughfare to its present width. As a result of the road works, the tramway was relaid, using

Brush-built cars in Castle Meadow before widening took place.
Photo: Neal's of Norwich

new rails, the reconstructed tramway coming into operation on 27th January, 1927. The same year saw the introduction of another bus service:

> Service 3—City to "Heartsease" public house, Plumstead Road, via Thorpe Station and Quebec Road; operated every 12 minutes.

In 1928 the company reintroduced (or revised—it has not been possible to establish the precise circumstances) the system of privilege tickets to workers of limited means. Under this scheme any person who could establish that his earnings did not exceed 40s. per week (the maximum before the 1914–18 war had been 25s.) was allowed 22 journeys weekly over the normal 2d. stages for 2s. 6d.

A new shelter was erected in Orford Place during 1928 at a cost of £650. It was a metal structure and was built by Walter Macfarlane and Company of Glasgow. On 18th February, 1929, F. Buckley succeeded Jewell as manager of the Norwich Electric Tramways Company. On

The tram shelter in Orford Place.   *Photo: G. Plunkett*

147

1st June, 1929, Messrs. Fitt Bros. started a bus service from All Saints Green to Lakenham. Later, the same operators introduced a service from All Saints Green to Tuckswood.

The next tramway to be abandoned was from Orford Place to City Road, ceasing operation on 24th March, 1930. On the following day, bus service 3 was extended via Queen's Road and City Road to Lakenham, Cavell Road—one wonders whether this was as a result of Fitt Bros.' venture in 1929. The company service was operated every 12 minutes on weekdays, using four buses, and every ten minutes on Saturdays, using five buses. On the same day, 25th March, 1930, a new bus service 7 commenced operation between Chapel Field Road and The Avenues. Bus service 6 between St. Andrew's Plain and Turner Road via Heigham Street commenced on 2nd August, 1930. During September, 1930, work commenced on the relaying of the rails in Magdalen Street. A significant event had occurred on 8th August, 1930, when a demonstration covered-top double-deck bus was tried out on the Mile Cross service. As a result, on 1st November, 1930, covered-top double-deck buses were introduced on the service to Aylsham Road. These vehicles were Leyland TD1's, with 48 seats, fleet numbers 28–31.

It should be noted that on the common sections where tramway cars and buses operated, or where buses had replaced the tramway services, the fares remained the same. By 1929–30 the tramway maximum fare was 3½d., which covered a cross-city journey from Eaton terminus (Newmarket Road) to the Cavalry Barracks or from Earlham terminus to Thorpe Road terminus, except that when cars ran to Mousehold Heath an additional 1d. was charged for the final section and the through journey from Eaton cost 4½d. Intermediate fares were 1d., 1½d., 2d., 2½d., and 3d.

At this date the services operated were:

Eaton—Cavalry Barracks
Cars operated at 10-minute intervals.

Dereham Road—Royal Hotel
On Mondays to Fridays cars operated every 8 minutes until 1 p.m., then every 7½ minutes until 9.15 p.m., then every 8 minutes to finish. On Saturdays, cars operated as above (Monday–Friday) until 12 noon, then every 6 minutes to finish.

Earlham Road—Thorpe Road
Cars operated on Mondays to Fridays at 6-minute intervals; Satur-

148

days at 5-minute intervals; Sundays at $7\frac{1}{2}$-minute intervals to 2.15 p.m., 6-minute intervals until 7 p.m., and 5-minute intervals to finish.

Unthank Road—Magdalen Road
Cars operated on Mondays–Fridays at 5-minute intervals, until 9 p.m., then every 6 minutes; Saturdays at 5-minute intervals; Sundays at 6-minute intervals to 6.30 p.m., then at 5-minute intervals to finish.

Trowse Station—Orford Place
Cars operated every 30 minutes.

City Road—Orford Place
Cars operated at 30-minute intervals.

Services on weekdays commenced between 6.30 a.m. and 7 a.m., finishing at 11.30 p.m.; on Sundays the services commenced at 10.15 a.m. (except to Trowse and City Road, which services commenced at 11.30 a.m.) and finished as on weekdays.

TRANSFER TICKETS, available on day of issue only

Thorpe Station and Unthank Road	
,, ,, ,, Earlham Road	
,, ,, ,, Dereham Road	$2\frac{1}{2}$d.
,, ,, ,, Golf Links	
,, ,, ,, City Road	
,, ,, ,, Trowse	
Thorpe Station and Magdalen Road 2d.	

Tickets were punched in the alighting stage number; e.g. for St. Giles to Orford Place, the ticket was punched in stage 6. However, any Victoria Station ticket was punched in stage 11.

At this time the *principal* fares on the bus services were as follows:

Duke Street to Boundary Inn—2d. single, 3d. return.
Duke Street to "The Firs"—4d. single, 6d. return.
Queen Street and Drayton Road—2d. single.
Orford Place and Harvey Lane—$2\frac{1}{2}$d. single.
Orford Place and Cavell Road—$1\frac{1}{2}$d. single.
Harvey Lane and Cavell Road—4d. single.
Earlham tram terminus and Jessop Road—$1\frac{1}{2}$d.
Earlham tram terminus and Fiveways—1d.

Earlham tram terminus and Golf Links—1½d.
TRANSFER TICKET—tram and bus, Orford Place and Golf
   Links—3d.
Queen Street and Dereham Road—2d.
Queen Street and Larkman Lane—3d.
Wall Road and Castle Meadow—2½d.
Castle Meadow and The Avenues—1½d.
Corbet Avenue and Orford Place—3d.
Orford Place and The Avenues—2d.

Children under three years of age free; three years and under twelve, half fare. Minimum fare 1d.; fraction of ½d.—½d.

Workpeople's fares in operation at the time were as follows:

Summer
1st March to 31st October up to 8.30 a.m., between 12.30 p.m. and 2.30 p.m., and between 5 p.m. and 7.15 p.m.

Winter
1st November to 28th February up to 8.30 a.m., between 12.30 p.m. and 2.30 p.m., and between 4.30 p.m. and 7.15 p.m.

These tickets were not available on Sundays, Bank Holidays, or after 2 p.m. on Saturdays.

1d. workmen's single journey tickets available over any ordinary 2d. tram stage.

2d. and 2½d. workmen's return tickets available on day of issue only.

2d. workmen's return tickets available over any 2d. tram stage and one return journey over same stage during the above-stated hours.

2½d. workmen's return tickets available over any ordinary 2½d. tram stage and one return journey over the same stage during the above-stated hours.

Originally, and until 1930, dogs were not allowed inside cars or buses, but after 1930 dogs which were under proper control and in the charge of passengers were allowed to travel at a charge of 1d. per dog per single journey. In the case of double-deck buses, dogs were permitted on the upper deck only, and small dogs only were permitted on single-deck buses.

Specimen tickets used on the Norwich Electric Tramways.

In line with increases in passenger fares, the charges for the conveyance of unaccompanied parcels had risen and, furthermore, the charges were now varied in accordance with the weight of the parcel.

Parcels Express

Parcels were conveyed within the city (i.e. of Norwich) and parcels could be handed to the conductor of any car or bus for delivery, or could be handed into the Parcels Office, Orford Hill, at the following rates:

Up to 3 lb.—3d.	Up to 21 lb.—6d.	Up to 56 lb.—9d.
„ „ 7 lb.—4d.	„ „ 28 lb.—7d.	„ „ 84 lb.—1s. 2d.
„ „ 14 lb.—5d.	„ „ 42 lb.—8d.	„ „ 112 lb.—1s. 6d.

There was also a 6d. (green) insurance ticket which meant that the parcel was insured against loss, damage, etc., and which was purchased in addition to the usual parcel ticket.

The company also owned a bicycle for delivery of parcels from the office on Timber Hill, and later a motor parcels van was purchased.

In 1930 the Special Committee appointed by the City Council to examine the problems of passenger transport in Norwich recommended to the City Council:

> That steps be taken in any Bill to be promoted by the Corporation in Parliament to secure powers to the Corporation to run a municipal bus service in the city.

This was one of the recommendations of the report which dealt with a number of other subjects besides the tramways, but the Committee's conclusions relating to the tramways which preceded the above recommendation are of interest. They were:

(a) No extension of the present tramway system is desirable on the main internal traffic routes of the city, as your Committee are of the opinion that the tramways are a source of congestion in the streets of the city.

(b) Having regard to the cost involved, the acquisition of the tramways by the Corporation is not a practical proposition on the basis laid down in the Tramways Act.

The purchase powers in the Norwich Electric Tramways Act, 1897, may be summarised as being 35 years after the date of the Act, and thereafter at intervals of seven years. If the Corporation acquired the undertaking before the expiration of 50 years from the passing of the Act (1897), they were required to pay the then value of the undertaking as a going concern, and in addition a part of the cost of new streets and street widenings carried out under the local Tramways Acts. If, however, they decided to purchase the undertaking after the 50 years from 1897, they could do so by paying the then value of the tramway and all lands, buildings, works, materials and plant appertaining thereto. This report set the stage for five eventful years, as the year in which the purchase powers could be next exercised was 1932.

On 20th February, 1931, the company announced that improved tramway cars would come into service in Norwich, but the company was proceeding with the development of its bus services, and on 30th March, 1933, bus service 7 was extended from Chapel Field Road, via Castle Meadow, Colegate, Pitt Street, Aylsham Road and Philadelphia Lane to Wall Road; two A.E.C. Regent double-deck vehicles with Park Royal 52-seat bodies were delivered for the opening of the service, which was operated at 30-minute intervals. Later in the same year the last bus service to be opened by the company as an independent company—service 17—came into operation between The Avenues and Mousehold Lane (Corbet Avenue) via The Avenues, Chapel Field, Castle Meadow, Thorpe Road, Quebec Road, Plumstead Road and Heartsease Lane. It operated with two buses at intervals of 30 minutes.

In 1932 six Leyland TD2 double-deck vehicles with Leyland 48-seat high-bridge bodies were delivered, the last buses to be delivered to the Norwich Electric Tramways Company as such, because, as mentioned above, in 1932 the Corporation's 35 years compulsory purchase powers became effective and there followed a year of uncertainty regarding the future of the company.

Although certain members of the City Council were against the purchase of the company, the City Council decided to go ahead with the proposed acquisition, and on 30th November, 1932, Norwich Corporation promoted a Bill to authorise the Corporation to acquire and operate the tramway and omnibus undertakings of the Norwich Electric Tramways Company and to authorise the Corporation to borrow money for the purchase of the undertaking, and also to abandon the tramways and to substitute buses.

A public meeting held in Norwich on 21st December, 1932, at the St. Andrew's Hall, rejected by 314 votes to 275 the Corporation's proposal to purchase the company. Among the objectors was the Ratepayers Association. Herbert Witard, a former Lord Mayor, spoke in support of the purchase. Feeling began to run so strongly in Norwich that a Tramway Opposition Committee was organised with C. R. Bignold as Chairman and R. P. Braund as organiser. At the same time, spurred on by the controversy that sprang up over the proposed purchase of the tramway company, local residents began to call for the replacement of the trams by buses in any event, whether the company remained independent or passed into the control of the Corporation. A City Council meeting on 31st December, 1932, decided to have a poll of citizens over the purchase. At this meeting there were angry exchanges and animated scenes during the tramways purchase discussion.

The local newspapers were full of letters, both supporting and opposing the proposal, and public meetings were called with speakers for both sides of the case. The polling day was set for Tuesday, 10th January, 1933, and as the day approached it was not unlike election time, with the Tramways Opposition Committee publishing leaflets giving their interpretation of the financial position and how they considered the ratepayers would be affected. The City Council proposed to purchase the Norwich Electric Tramways Company for £175,000 and hoped to show an annual profit of £3,500 if the undertaking was run as a bus-operated concern. It was also the view of the Corporation that it would be unwise for them to allow the control of traffic in the city to be handed over to any other private undertaking, and they considered it was a matter into which they should go themselves. The Corporation consulted A. R. Fearnley, General Manager of Sheffield Corporation Tramways, who went thoroughly into the proposed purchase. Fearnley and the City Accountant, after much consideration, recommended that the Corporation should purchase the tramway undertaking which, in their opinion, would have been a sound business venture.

It was stated by the Tramways Opposition Committee that a vote against the purchase would mean that:

1. The tramway company would be forced to make the change-over themselves without any cost to the ratepayers at all: or,
2. The tramway company might sell to another transport undertaking who would in their own interests change over from trams to buses immediately.

As the campaign hotted up, the Tramways Opposition Committee distributed 90,000 pamphlets, and ten sandwich-men paraded the streets on their behalf. And so it went on with meetings, leading articles in

154

No. 43 at Orford Place; an English Electric Company body on an ex-trailer car truck.

Photo: M. J. O'Connor

No. 6 at Earlham Road terminus. A typical tramway view.

Photo: C. R. Temple

the newspapers, letters to editors, and so on. On polling day the result was known by 9.30 p.m.: 11,033 against the purchase and 7,775 for purchase, only 29 per cent of the local government electors having voted. Afterwards there was an anti-climax; a few letters appeared in the newspapers about the result, but the next development did not come for nearly twelve months.

What was to be the Norwich Electric Tramways Company's last annual report was dated 30th June, 1933, and it showed total receipts of £113,350 16s. 2d. as against expenses of £95,921 13s. 2d., a net profit of £17, 429 3s.

It was not until the end of 1933 that the future of the company became known to the public when, on 1st December, 1933, the Eastern Counties Omnibus Company Limited announced that they had obtained a controlling interest in the Norwich Electric Tramways Company, as a result of which 44 tramway cars, 33 buses, a motor parcels van and various premises came under the control of the Eastern Counties Omnibus Company Limited.

A Leyland TS1, rebuilt as a double-decker.

Photo: Eastern Counties Omnibus Company Ltd.

Early in 1934 the Chairman of the Eastern Counties Omnibus Company Limited announced that it was his company's intention to abandon the tramways in favour of buses at the earliest possible moment. This was no great surprise to the citizens of Norwich, and the local Press supported the move. The Bill for abandonment was promoted on 26th November, 1934.

During this time the Norwich Electric Tramways Company retained its separate identity, and in the summer of 1934 five vehicles acquired by the Eastern Counties Omnibus Company received new bodies before they were passed over to the Norwich Electric Tramways Company fleet, in which they were numbered 48–52. One of the unhappy events of 1934 was the death of Buckley, the General Manager of the Norwich Electric Tramways Company.

Passengers carried, 1932–1934

| | 1932 | | 1933 | | 1934 | |
	TRAMS	BUSES	TRAMS	BUSES	TRAMS	BUSES
No. of car miles run	1,168,012	808,643	1,166,325	925,711	1,138,261	981,218
No. of passengers carried	12,475,731	6,214,187	11,751,617	6,502,034	11,254,247	7,289,912
Earnings per car mile	15.52d.	11.51d.	14.60d.	11.00d.	14.22d.	11.64d.
Expenses per car mile	11.42d.	8.73d.	11.27d.	8.33d.	10.85d.	8.76d.
Earnings per passenger	1.39d.	1.49d.	1.39d.	1.55d.	1.39d.	1.55d.

On 5th February, 1935, the Norwich Electric Tramways Bill was read for the first time and it received the Royal Assent on 6th June, 1935. The "Norwich Electric Tramways Act, 1935" provided for:

(a) The abandonment of the tramways.

(b) The substitution of buses for the tramways.

(c) Changing the company's name to the "Norwich Omnibus Company."

(d) The company had to give notice to the Corporation within two years of the passing of the Act that the whole of the tramways would be abandoned.

(e) The company was required to pay to the Corporation £32,000; this payment relieved the company of any responsibility for the maintenance of the roads in which the rails were situated after the tramways were abandoned. In other words, the Corporation became responsible for lifting the rails and dismantling the overhead line equipment, the material becoming their property.

(f) Section 42 of the Act stated:

"As from the passing of this Act (i.e. Norwich Electric Tramways Act, 1935) section 43 (Future purchase of undertaking by local authority) of the Tramways Act, 1870, shall cease to apply to the undertaking of the Company (Norwich Omnibus Company) or any part thereof."

There were other sections as to the financial, administrative and legal aspects of the new company.

It was arranged that vehicles delivered from the passing of the Norwich Electric Tramways Act, 1935, would be Eastern Counties Omnibus Company vehicles in their familiar livery of scarlet and cream, operating on hire to the Norwich Omnibus Company. From 1935 onwards the Norwich Omnibus Company vehicles were progressively renumbered (see schedule at end of chapter) and repainted in the Eastern Counties livery and, with the exception of one vehicle, all vehicles carried the legal owners' name as Eastern Counties Omnibus Company Limited. The exception was a vehicle which had "Norwich Omnibus Company" as legal owner.

Final abandonment of the tramways was now near, and on 27th July, 1935, the tramway services between Dereham Road and Royal Hotel and between Thorpe Road and Earlham Road were replaced by bus services. New bus service 14 (later 81), combining Eastern Counties service 13A and the Dereham Road tramway service, commenced operating every seven minutes between Dereham (Oval) and Thorpe railway station, using five buses.

The Thorpe Road–Earlham Road tramway service (a six-minute service requiring nine tramway cars) was replaced by a new bus service 80 from Thorpe (Harvey Lane) to Earlham (Fiveways) incorporating the tramway service and feeder service 5 from Earlham tram terminus to Fiveways. The new service operated every seven minutes using eight buses.

The Unthank Road–Magdalen Road tramway service was, in 1935, operated as follows:

Every 5 minutes during the "off-peak" periods, using 12 cars.
Every 4 minutes during "peak" periods, using 15 cars.

No. 12 (a Brush car which survived with No. 5 to the end of tramway operation) at St. Catherine's Plain. *Photo: G. Plunkett*

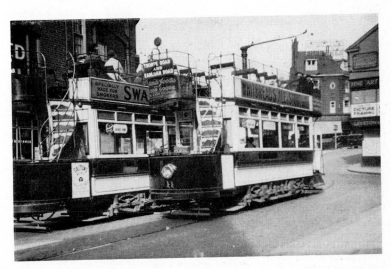

No. 11 in Orford Place. *Photo: M. J. O'Connor*

This service was replaced by buses on 21st November, 1935, the last tramway car operating on 20th November. The replacement bus service, 89, was introduced between Unthank Road (Judges Walk) and Wall Road; The Avenues–Wall Road service (Norwich Omnibus Company service 7) was diverted at Tombland via Palace Street and Silver Road to Sprowston (Blue Boar).

The last tramway service was from Newmarket Road to Cavalry Barracks (operated at intervals of ten minutes, using five cars) and it ceased on 10th December, 1935, bus service 90 taking over next day, when it was extended to Cringleford using five single-deck buses to operate a ten-minute service.

Car No. 10 was the last car and it ran from Orford Place to Eaton and back to the car sheds in Silver Road. The car commenced its journey from Orford Place at 11.10 p.m. and was cheered off by a

No. 10, the last Norwich tram, photographed in Silver Road depôt, 10th December, 1935.

Photo: Neal's of Norwich.

160

crowd of 500 people who had gathered in Orford Place for the occasion. When the car started, there was a rush which packed the car both inside and outside, including the conductor's platform.

As the car moved off, the crowd cheered and people in Newmarket Road stood at their gateways to see the car on its last journey. The passengers on the car sang "Auld Lang Syne" for the twelfth time as it reached Eaton terminus. On the return journey, the tram was followed by a trail of motor cars and bicycles, and at the car sheds in Silver Road there was another cheering crowd who sang "Auld Lang Syne" for the thirty-sixth time.

The last car was driven by George Hill, the longest-serving driver, with 37 years' service with the Norwich Electric Tramways Company. The conductor, B. Fisher, was the youngest conductor—at that time— employed by the Norwich Electric Tramways Company.

On the last days of tramway operation, Norwich Omnibus Company tickets had been issued on the cars.

The rails were progressively lifted by Corporation workmen and the overhead standards were mostly removed, although a few still remain; particularly the set in Magpie Road which are used for street lighting. The car sheds, after serving as a NAAFI base depôt during the war, are used as a warehouse by a firm of food distributors, and the bus garage erected at the rear of the car sheds is still in use by the Eastern Counties Omnibus Company Limited for the storage of vehicles and other equipment, but it has not been used as a garage for many years.

Fourteen trolley standards from the cars were used as fence posts at a house near the depôt. Two of them were purchased in 1963 by the author acting on behalf of enthusiasts who required them for use in connection with restoration of tramway cars for museum purposes.

Stoppages of the tramway services had been very rare, but two notable occasions (probably the only two) are on record. The first was due to an exceptionally heavy snowfall one Christmas/Boxing Day night which caused part of the service to be suspended. Another difficulty arose in late August, 1912, when torrential rain caused the flooding of the power station and put it out of action. On that occasion the Lakenam and Trowse bridges were breached. Services also ceased from 4th May to 12th May, 1926, during the General Strike, believed to be the sole occasion when labour troubles interfered with operation.

161

Norwich city bus services, as operated by the Eastern Counties Omnibus Company Limited following the closure of the tramways, were:

Service	80	Harvey Lane (Morse Avenue)—Thorpe Station—Colman Road (short workings, Thorpe Station to Earlham—Fiveways)
,,	81	Costessey (Oval)—Dereham Road—Thorpe Station
,,	82	Harvey Lane (Morse Avenue)—Thorpe Station—Lakenham (Cavell Road)
,,	83	Trowse (White Horse)—Royal Hotel—Dereham Road—Larkman Lane
,,	84	Jessop Road—The Avenues—Tombland—Sprowston (Blue Boar)
,,	85	Blue Bell Road—The Avenues—Thorpe Station—Ketts Hill—Harvey Lane (Morse Avenue) or Corbet Avenue (Mousehold Lane)
,,	86/87	Duke Street—Mile Cross—Middleton Lane—The Firs
,,	88	All Saints Green or Thorpe Station—Royal Hotel—City Station—Drayton Road
,,	89	Unthank Road (Judges Walk)—Tombland—Wall Road (short workings, Orford Place—Wall Road)
,,	90	Eaton (Church Lane)—Orford Place—Nelson Barracks
,,	91*	Thorpe Station—Tombland—Sprowston (Blue Boar)
,,	92†	Mile Cross (Boundary Inn)—Catton Grove—Thorpe Station—Thorpe (St. Andrew's Hospital)
,,	93‡	Thorpe Station—Old Catton

Notes

Services 80–90 inclusive were those previously operated by the Norwich Electric Tramways Company and their successors the Norwich Omnibus Company.

* Service 91 was ex-Eastern Counties Omnibus Company Limited service 8A.

† Service 92 was ex-Eastern Counties Omnibus Company Limited service 7A, and was the only purely city service operated by the Eastern Counties Omnibus Company in tramway days.

‡ Service 93 was ex-Eastern Counties Omnibus Company Limited service 8, and was renumbered 93 and grouped with the city services when they were taken over by the Eastern Counties Omnibus Company.

The two services operated by Fitt Bros. were acquired by the Eastern Counties Omnibus Company in October, 1939.

On 16th February, 1936, the residents of Newmarket Road entertained a large number of men who had served as motormen or conductors on the tramways, with their wives, to a dinner and entertainment at Ashworth and Pikes restaurant, Norwich—a very nice gesture.

The board of the Norwich Omnibus Company was formed of members of the City Council and of the Eastern Counties Omnibus Company Limited. The Norwich Omnibus Company remained in existence until 1955 when it was dissolved, even though the Eastern Counties Omnibus Company Limited had passed into British Transport Commission control in 1948.

The main city picking-up point is in Castle Meadow; Orford Place is now a pedestrian way as it was considerably narrowed when the area around was rebuilt as a result of damage caused by bombing during the 1939–1945 war.

Schedule of cars
The cars delivered to the Norwich Electric Tramways Company followed the standard British practice of the time and were all double-deck open-top four-wheel cars mounted on 6 ft.-wheelbase Peckham Cantilever trucks with 30-inch diameter wheels; the trucks were supplied by R. W. Blackwell and Company. Each car had two Westinghouse 25-h.p. motors (with the exception of 7, 9, 16, 32 and 36 which had two 30-h.p. motors), Westinghouse 28A controllers, centre trolleys with Winslow's (Winslow was engineer of the New General Traction Company) patent interior spring and fixed heads. The 28A controllers had seven notches, four series and three parallel, and motormen were instructed that they must not run for longer than two minutes on other than the "preferred running points" numbers four and seven. Main motor switches and lightning arresters were supplied by the Westinghouse Company, but no electric brakes were fitted; there were hand wheel brakes only; slipper brakes were fitted at a later date. All motor cars were supplied with drawbars for hauling trailer cars.

The bodies, by the Brush Electrical Engineering Co., had seating for 26 persons inside and 26 outside; the outside seats were of the garden-seat type with seat covers, and the inside seats were of the wooden longitudinal pattern with rugs for upholstery. There were five arched windows each side with pull-down blinds, quarter-turn stairs, wire netting from roof level to the centre top-deck guard rail, small destina-

No. 35, an original Brush car, at Thorpe 'Redan' public house.

A Peckham truck of the Norwich Electric Tramways Company.

tion indicator boxes (the destination was displayed by means of an inserted slide on which was painted the name of the terminal destination) and "bull's-eye" lamps with a colour code for indicating the service during hours of darkness. The overall length was 29 ft., length inside 17 ft. 6 in., overall width 6 ft., and height inside 6 ft. 6 in.

During hours of darkness, lighting was provided for passengers by six interior electric lamps and four electric lamps on the top deck. Road lighting was provided by oil head and tail lamps hung over the dash. These lamps were independent of the cars and were brought down daily from the depôt to Orford Place. Passengers were not permitted to smoke inside the car or in front of the trolley standard (the front depending on the direction of travel of the car).

The first 40 motor cars were numbered 1–40 and were delivered direct to the Norwich Electric Tramways Company in 1900 by the British Westinghouse Company who acted as contractors but not car builders; ten similar trailer cars, numbered 41–50, were delivered at about the same time. These trailer cars were similar to the motor cars, except that they were shorter (four windows each side instead of five) and had seating for only 40 persons. Trailer cars were operated on the service to Trowse and to Mousehold on occasions of heavy traffic, as for instance on Bank Holidays. In service, the maximum speed for all cars, as set by the Board of Trade, was ten miles per hour.

It is suggested that there was also a water-tank car.

Experience indicated that the small destination boxes were not entirely suitable, and as a result in 1904 destination boards were hung from the top-deck rails above the destination boxes.

In 1905 two cars were acquired from the Coventry Electric Tramways Company (another New General Traction Company undertaking) in which fleet they were numbered 19 and 20. As no records now survive, it is presumed that they were numbered 41 and 42 in the Norwich Electric Tramways Company fleet and that the trailer cars with these numbers were renumbered 51 and 52. (While this cannot be established from records, enquiries indicate that this is what did, in fact, happen.) The ex-Coventry cars were the same in appearance as Nos. 1–40.

During 1906, the wire-netting was replaced by decency boards, additional lifeguards were fitted, and slipper brakes installed. This work was carried out on all motor cars and, with the exception of the slipper brakes which were installed later, on all trailer cars.

A reciprocal transfer took place in 1910 when the Norwich Electric Tramways Company cars Nos. 7, 9, 16, 32 and 36 were transferred to the Coventry Electric Tramways Company, in which fleet they were renumbered 37–41. The Coventry Electric Tramways Company fitted the cars with canopies, thereby increasing the outside seating to 34; in addition, the cars were retrucked with Peckham Pendulum P22 trucks, and Westinghouse "200" 30-h.p. motors were installed. In 1930 Coventry No. 38 (ex-Norwich No. 16) was fitted with new Dick, Kerr type DB1-K3 controllers and upholstered on the lower deck.

The trailer cars were unpopular with the motormen, as they tended to jump the points and at terminals it was necessary for the motor car to run around the trailer (an examination of the map will show that the terminal loops were installed with a view to trailer car operation), uncoupling and coupling as necessary—this was not a popular practice in wet weather. As a result of the experience gained over the first years of operation, it was decided in 1907 to abandon trailer operation. Five of the cars were stored (Nos. 48–52) and the remaining five (Nos. 43–47) were fitted with electrical equipment and converted to motor cars for use on the Aylsham Road service. Nos. 48–52 were scrapped during the First World War. In 1908 Nos. 7, 9, 16, 32 and 36 were fitted with Mountain and Gibson trucks; No. 32 certainly had a Mountain and Gibson radial truck.

No. 32, mounted on the Mountain and Gibson radial truck.

No. 46 was the "track car" in that special emery blocks were fitted into the slipper brake shoes which were screwed down for track grinding. No. 47 was used for pushing the snow plough, but when this car received a new English Electric body in 1924, No. 46 undertook the snow plough duties. The snow plough was a separate unit mounted on four wheels.

During 1912–14 the height of the top-deck guard rails was increased on all cars, which also received electric head and tail lamps in place of the oil lamps. The year 1914 also saw the first appearance of advertisements on the rocker panels.

During the First World War, as mentioned above, the Norwich Aerodrome extension was opened, and in this connection the Norwich Electric Tramways Company acquired from the British Thomson-Houston Company of Rugby four 37/40 h.p. GE 249 motors, two pairs of B49 controllers and electrical equipment which, with two ordinary Peckham four-wheel trucks, was used to construct two motorised goods wagons. These were constructed at Silver Road car sheds and, when finished, resembled railway trucks with end platforms on which were mounted the controllers and handbrake stanchions. For weather protection for the motormen there was an awning over the platform. A reinforced girder was placed longitudinally between the two bulkheads, and the trolley was mounted on this girder ; incidentally, the truck frames were of 7 ft. wheelbase instead of the standard 6 ft., in order to accommodate the larger motors. The controllers incorporated a special push-button brake. Apparently the wagons were very fast and are alleged to have been capable of exceeding 30 miles per hour; riding is said to have been steady on curves, despite the lengthened wheelbase.

Immediately after the First World War, the rugs on the inside seats were removed, as were the covers on the outside seats. The post-war fleet consisted of 42 cars (52 acquired, ten disposed of), and it was increased in 1923 by two additional cars which utilised the trucks, motors, controllers and equipment from the two wagons (ex-Mousehold Aerodrome tramway), these having been handed over to the Norwich Electric Tramways Company at the cessation of hostilities. Various modifications were carried out to the equipment from the wagons and the push-button brake was removed. The bodies for these cars were built by the English Electric Company and were of improved design (although they remained open-top), having four windows per side, longitudinal wooden seating inside, close slat lift-over seats outside, and half-turn staircases. These bodies were uncanopied, as it was considered that the weight of the extended canopies and additional passengers would prove excessive for the short-wheelbase trucks. (It should be remembered that the Coventry cars which were canopied had long-wheelbase Mountain and Gibson trucks, in place of the original Peckham Cantilever trucks.) The seating was 26 inside and 29 outside. These rebuilt cars were given the numbers 7 and 9, which numbers had been carried by two of the cars sold to the Coventry Electric Tramways Company in 1910.

Following on from these rebuilds, a number of the Brush-bodied cars were rebuilt using the original Peckham trucks and the Westinghouse motors, but new English Electric Company controllers with eight notches, four series and four parallel, and rheostatic brakes (certain cars had the controllers mounted on a raised platform above the crown-board) and English Electric equipment, together with English Electric bodies of the same pattern as used for cars Nos. 7 and 9. This rebuilding programme extended from 1923 to 1930; the first two batches were supplied at £685 each, the remainder at £695. Each order included the trolley bases, Hudson Bowring lifeguards, and controllers; these were of type K3B on the first twelve cars, K33B on the next twelve, and K33E on the last four. In all, 34 bodies were obtained from English Electric, as follows:

April, 1923	— 2	(Nos. 7 and 9)
May, 1924	— 4	(Nos. 43, 44, 45, 47)
December, 1924	— 6	(these and two cars of 1929 took numbers 4, 10, 11, 23, 30, 38, 39 and 41)
December, 1925	— 6	(Nos. 1, 2, 3, 8, 13, 24)
January, 1927	— 4	(Nos. 6, 17, 18, 29)
January, 1928	— 4	(Nos. 15, 25, 40, 42)
March, 1929	— 4	(Nos. 14, 33 and two of the eight listed under December, 1924)
January, 1930	— 2	(Nos. 20 and 26)
August, 1930	— 2	(Nos. 22 and 34)

A summary of rebodied cars is as follows:

Rebodied: Nos. 1-4, 6-11, 13-15, 17, 18, 20, 22-26, 29, 30, 33, 34, 38-42 and ex-motorised trailers 43-45 and 47.
Not rebodied: Nos. 5, 12, 19, 21, 27, 28, 31, 35, 37 and ex-motorised trailer 46. This excludes the cars which went to Coventry.

The first new English Electric bodies were fitted with roller blind destination indicators set above the top-deck guard rails, but in 1930

Right: No. 41, a new English Electric Company body and, it is believed, an ex-Coventry car's truck. *Photo: English Electric Company Ltd.*

Below: No. 9, one of the English Electric Company bodies mounted on one of the ex-powered wagon trucks.
Photo: G. Plunkett

No. 15, a new English Electric Company body with high front destination indicators.
Photo: English Electric Company Ltd.

The interior of an English Electric Company body.
Photo: English Electric Company Ltd.

the destination boxes were removed and the company reverted to the practice of having a coloured board fitted above the front decency screen. The board was illuminated during hours of darkness. A number of the English Electric bodies had roller blind destination boxes fitted inside the lower saloon, while others had the standard short-length side boards. Under the canopies there was a pull-down flap with the word "FULL" painted on it. The final deliveries of the English Electric bodies had slightly longer canopies than those on the first new bodies, and they were delivered without the top destination boxes but with lower deck inside destination boxes; a neater lamp for top-deck illumination was also a feature of these later cars. A number of the English Electric bodies utilised top-deck lamps salvaged from scrapped Brush bodies. The English Electric bodies had considerably higher top-deck rails than the Brush bodies.

By 1932 the "bull's-eye" destination boxes finally disappeared from all Brush cars and the top destination board was illuminated in the same manner as that on the English Electric bodies.

The livery of the Norwich Electric Tramways Company was maroon and white. The upper waist panels, dashes, ventilator boards and upper side panels were maroon; the window frames, corner panels, decency boards (where no advertisements were displayed) and lower rocker

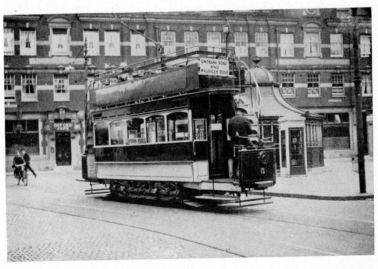

Photographed in 1932, this illustration depicts the final appearance of the Brush cars.   Photo: M. J. O'Connor

Rebodied No. 38 in Orford Place.

Photo: H. B. Priestley

panels were white. The maroon panels had double lining-out in gold
on the dashes and rocker panels and single gold lines on the ventilator
and upper side panels. The ivory panels were lined out in maroon and
the fleet number was carried on the dash in large gold numbers shaded
in red and silver, and on the centre waist panel in smaller unshaded gold
numbers. Above the ventilator boards, the company's name "NOR-
WICH ELECTRIC TRAMWAYS COMPANY" was displayed in five-
inch gold letters. Truck frames were initially cherry red and latterly
black; the decency boards were white, lined out in black, and painted
advertisements, of the usual enamelled type, were normally carried on
them. On the Brush bodies these advertisements extended the full
length of the side of the car. In the early days, these cars had advertisements painted on the outer stair stringers. Various cars had advertisements on the rocker panels, and these advertisements were always in
maroon or black lettering, to tone with the car's livery.

172

When the English Electric bodies were delivered, the company's name was no longer displayed on the upper side panel but was in smaller lettering set in an oval band on the waist panel, and the number was in the centre of the band. Single gold lines replaced the double gold lines on the waist panels and dashes. The remaining Brush-bodied cars were "decked-out" in the same manner as they were overhauled and repainted.

Towards the final cessation of tramway operation, various advertisement contracts expired and a number of the Brush cars appeared with ivory painted decency panels. At the same time, advertisements on the rocker panels were gradually removed for the same reason.

As was usual practice, the interior of the cars featured polished woodwork, the English Electric bodies having on each side light ventilators which in a number of cases had advertisements transferred on from the inside.

Company cars were always well turned out and kept in a good clean state of repair.

When tramway operation finally ceased in December, 1935, it was possible to purchase car bodies, less trucks and glass, for £5 each.

Schedule of buses

Until the formation of the Norwich Omnibus Company, the original fleet numbers were retained and five vehicles were added to the Norwich Electric Tramways Company stock in 1934, after having been purchased from Varsity Express Coaches Limited by the Eastern Counties Omnibus Company Limited.

The Norwich Electric Tramways Company vehicles were painted in a reddish-brown (known as Norwich tramways red) and ivory; lettering and fleet numbers were in gold leaf. The crest and fleet number were carried on the lower side panels. The company's name was set out in the oval band and the vehicle's fleet number was in the centre.

Vehicles delivered after 1935 were painted in the standard Eastern Counties Omnibus Company livery of scarlet and cream and, as mentioned above, operated on hire to the Norwich Omnibus Company. The Norwich Omnibus Company vehicles were progressively repainted in the Eastern Counties Omnibus Company livery. Over the course of the years, the original vehicles were in many cases rebodied or rebuilt and re-engined, but this does not form part of the history of the Norwich

Electric Tramways Company, and for anyone interested, full details are contained in Omnibus Society/P.S.V. Circle publication No. P.F.1, which gives a detailed history of the fleet of the Eastern Counties Omnibus Company Limited.

The last Norwich Electric Tramways Company vehicles to see service with the Eastern Counties Omnibus Company were LG4 and LG6, which were converted in 1952 to permanent open-top vehicles for use on the Felixstowe sea-front service. It is interesting to note that the original Weymann bodies—somewhat rebuilt, however—stayed on these chassis until the vehicles were withdrawn. LG4 (Norwich Electric Tramways Company No. 43) was sold in 1960 and LG6 (Norwich Electric Tramways Company No. 45) was sold in 1961.

Three Bristol 'B' type single-deck buses outside the bus depôt at Silver Road.

CHAPTER SEVEN

PIER TRAMWAYS, WISBECH AND UPWELL STEAM TRAMWAY, and LIGHT RAILWAYS

Coast Development Corporation Limited

THE name of this organisation occurs in connection with a number of tramway schemes for East Anglia, and it is for this reason that the Corporation's history is briefly outlined in this chapter.

For a number of years prior to 1900, various companies had operated regular steamer services during the summer between London and Great Yarmouth, and these services were a vital link in the transport arrangements for the conveyance of holidaymakers during the season. However, as a result of the failure in 1887 of the River Thames Steamship Co., some Clacton businessmen in conjunction with Dennys of Dumbarton (the famous shipbuilders) formed a new company, Belle Steamers Ltd., to operate passenger steamship services to serve the east coast as far north as Yarmouth. By 1898 it owned six paddle steamers, the Clacton Belle (1890), Woolwich Belle (1891), London Belle (1893), Southend Belle (1896), Walton Belle (1897), and Yarmouth Belle (1898). From this time until the outbreak of the First World War in 1914, the company operated the almost legendary Belle paddle steamers on their services from London to Great Yarmouth, Herne Bay and Ramsgate. Incidentally, the fares for the 11-hour voyage from London to the South Quay, Great Yarmouth, were 17s. 6d. return and 10s. single.

In 1898 a merger had taken place between Belle Steamers Ltd. and various other interests under the title of the Coast Development Company Ltd., registered on 7th January, 1898, "to develop any of the resources of the East Coast." The other constituents were the Clacton-on-Sea Pier Co., the Clacton-on-Sea and General Land Building and Investment Co. Ltd., the Clacton-on-Sea Hall and Library Ltd., and the Walton-on-the-Naze Pier and Hotel Co. Ltd. A further new steamer, the Southwold Belle, was added to the fleet in 1900.

During 1905 the company was reorganised as the Coast Development Corporation Ltd. and extended its activities by taking over the

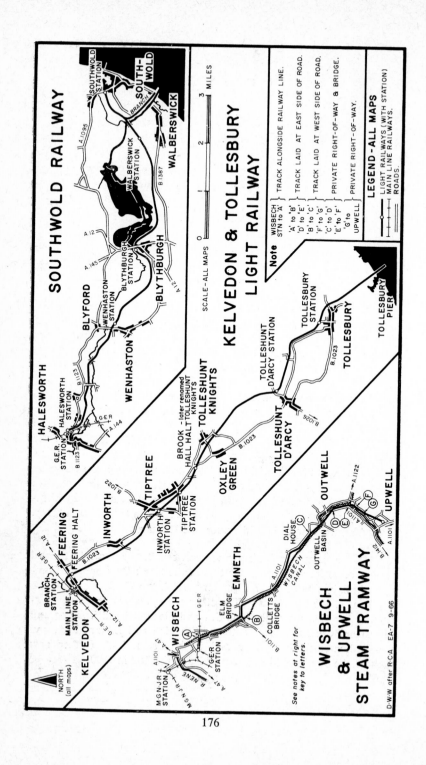

SOUTHWOLD RAILWAY

SOUTHWOLD

WALBERSWICK

HALESWORTH

BLYFORD

BLYTHBURGH

WENHASTON

SOUTHWOLD STATION

WALBERSWICK STATION

BLYTHBURGH STATION

WENHASTON STATION

HALESWORTH STATION

G.E.R. STATION

BRANCH

A.1095

B.1387

A.12

A.145

A.12

G.E.R.

A.144

B.1125

B.1123

NORTH (all maps)

SCALE—ALL MAPS

0   1   2   3
MILES

KELVEDON & TOLLESBURY LIGHT RAILWAY

KELVEDON

FEERING

INWORTH

TIPTREE

TOLLESHUNT KNIGHTS

OXLEY GREEN

TOLLESHUNT D'ARCY

TOLLESBURY

TOLLESBURY PIER

MAIN LINE STATION

BRANCH STATION

FEERING HALT

INWORTH STATION

TIPTREE STATION

BROOK – later renamed HALL HALT

TOLLESHUNT KNIGHTS

TOLLESHUNT D'ARCY STATION

TOLLESBURY STATION

G.E.R.

A.12

B.1022

B.1023

B.1023

B.1026

B.1023

B.1023

Note

WISBECH STN to 'A'	TRACK ALONGSIDE RAILWAY LINE.
'A' to 'B' 'D' to 'E'	TRACK LAID AT EAST SIDE OF ROAD.
'B' to 'C' 'F' to 'G'	TRACK LAID AT WEST SIDE OF ROAD.
'C' to 'D' 'E' to 'F'	PRIVATE RIGHT-OF-WAY & BRIDGE.
'G' to UPWELL	PRIVATE RIGHT-OF-WAY.

LEGEND - ALL MAPS

LIGHT RAILWAYS (WITH STATION)
MAIN LINE RAILWAYS.
ROADS.

WISBECH & UPWELL STEAM TRAMWAY

WISBECH

EMNETH

OUTWELL

UPWELL

ELM BRIDGE

COLLETTS BRIDGE

DIAL HOUSE

OUTWELL BASIN

WISBECH CANAL

G.E.R. STATION

M.G.N.J.R. STATION

R. NENE

See notes at right for key to letters.

A.1101

A.1101

A.1122

A.1101

A.47

A.47

A.1101

B.1412

G.E.R.

M.G.N.J.R.

D-W-W after R.C.A.   EA-7 9-66

176

piers at Lowestoft and Felixstowe and by providing electric light and power at Southwold and Walton, together with various hotels and housing schemes. At the outbreak of war in 1914 the steamers became minesweepers with the Royal Navy; the company went into liquidation in 1915, and when the services were resumed after the war it was under the auspices of a new company, the East Anglian Steamship Company, after which the Coast Development Corporation was finally wound up ; "thereby ended the existence of an organisation which had done much, and tried to do more, in the development of East Anglia." The steamers were gradually dispersed to other owners and trades, the last one (the former Walton Belle) being broken up as the Pride of Devon in 1951.

Felixstowe Pier Tramway

Projected in 1903 by the Coast Development Company Limited, the pier with its tramway was opened in August, 1905. The tramway used centre third rail current collection and was laid as a single track on the left-hand side of the pier (facing seawards) to a track gauge of 3 ft. 6 in. Rails of 36 lb. to the yard were used. Both pier and tramway were half a mile in length. Power was taken from Felixstowe Council's electricity works.

Originally three open-sided cross-bench toast-rack type cars, with a seating capacity given as 36 each, were used to operate the service

Felixstowe Pier Tramway in 1905, the year of opening.
Photo: Courtesy J. H. Price

L

which was provided only during the summer months. As there was no passing loop, cars worked in multiple unit. Conductors collected fares on the cars, using the Bell Punch ticket system; it is believed that the single fare in each direction was 3d.

The Coast Development Corporation Limited (who were the successors of the promoting company) went into liquidation in 1922 and the pier and tramway were acquired by East Coast Piers Limited who continued to run the tramway until 1939 when, as a result of the outbreak of war, the tramway service was suspended on 10th September, 1939, this time finally.

During 1940 the pier was severed as a defence measure, and during the war years it was damaged by the ravages of the sea, as a result of which the pier broke up. In 1947 a local company was formed to acquire the pier, following which in 1949 the remains of the old pier and tramway were demolished and a new, much shorter, pier built.

Schedule of cars

These were three in number (two motor cars and one trailer) but, unfortunately, it has not been possible to ascertain the name of the builder. These cars, which were painted brown and cream, were scrapped in 1931.

According to 'Light Railway and Tramway Journal,' the cars had Peckham trucks and Thomas Parker motors.

Felixstowe—the body of a pier railway car, photographed 18th May, 1952.
                                              Photo: J. H. Meredith

Latterly there was only one car and this consisted of the body of one of the original cars mounted on the truck of ex-Ipswich Corporation tramway car No. 34. The body of this car served as a waiting room at the Pier Head.

Walton-on-the-Naze Pier Tramway

Promoted and built by the Walton-on-the-Naze Pier and Hotel Co. Ltd., it was taken over by the Coast Development Company Limited, who opened it in August, 1898. The tramway was half a mile in length and was laid to a gauge of 3 ft. 6in. using 36 lb. to the yard rails. The centre third rail system of current collection was used and power for the three single-deck cars was obtained from a Parker's generator which developed 50 kilowatts. In operation the three cars ran as a train, there being no passing loops on the single track, although there was a siding at the Pier Head.

In 1935, the original tramway ceased operation and was replaced by a battery car running in a 6ft.-wide wooden trough. During 1937 the pier and battery car were purchased by the New Walton Pier Company Limited, but in 1942 the car was destroyed by fire. However, a 2 ft.-gauge railway, reviving rail traction, was laid in connection with the rebuilding of the pier, and in 1948 was adapted for the carriage of passengers.

Original rolling stock of the Walton-on-the-Naze Pier Tramway.

179

Fully-loaded cars on the Walton pier tramway.

The miniature railway, which uses an 0-4-0 diesel locomotive with a steam-outline superstructure, operates daily during the summer from Easter to October. The fare is 6d. return including pier toll.

The original rolling stock consisted of one motor car and two trailers; bodies were by the Ashbury Carriage and Iron Co., mounted on Peckham trucks with Crompton 15 h.p. motors in the motor car's truck.

The present rolling stock consists of the diesel locomotive mentioned above, which was built by Baguley of Burton-on-Trent, and three bogie toast-rack type coaches. The livery is red and white.

Wisbech and Upwell Steam Tramway

The first proposal for a rail link between Wisbech and Upwell came in 1873 when a man named Gillard obtained Parliamentary powers for a railway between Wisbech and Upwell, but due to difficulties in raising the necessary capital the scheme was not carried out.

In 1880 the Great Eastern Railway resurrected the scheme to link the two places but decided to reduce the construction and operating costs by constructing a tramway to be worked by steam locomotives within the provisions of the Tramways Act, 1870. The Act of Parliament, promoted in 1881, was passed and received the Royal Assent on 24th July, 1882.

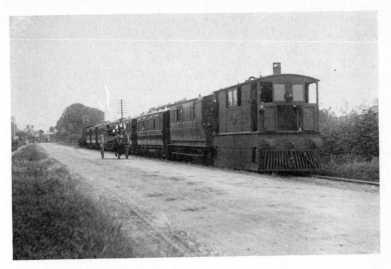

A train on the Wisbech and Upwell steam tramway in 1927.

Photo: K. A. C. R. Nunn

Construction was put in hand and on 20th August, 1883, the tramway was opened from Wisbech (G.E.R. station) to Outwell station, a distance of 4 miles and 10 chains. It is stated that 960 persons travelled on the tramway on the first day of operation. The extension onwards from Outwell station to Upwell was opened for traffic on 8th September, 1884, the overall distance between Wisbech and Upwell being 5 miles and 72 chains.

The tramway was laid to standard gauge from Wisbech along the bank of the former Wisbech canal until it reached Newcommon Bridge where it crossed the canal and the Elm Road–Ramnoth Road junction. Newcommon Bridge crossed the canal at the Royal Standard inn corner, and although the present-day bridge is a low-level concrete structure, it was, when the canal was in use, a hump-backed bridge which gave the tramway engines a difficult task. From here it followed the roadway and was, in places, laid in the public highway in which case the running rails were fitted with guard rails and the whole was embedded in the road surface so as to offer no obstruction to road vehicles. Originally this was done with cinder ballast but in later years road stone covered with tarmacadam was used.

After running alongside open fields, the tramway once more crossed the road at a point near the Duke of Wellington inn where a compulsory stop existed and continued to Elm Bridge depôt, which was situated on a bend opposite the road leading off to Emneth. The tramway

181

then followed the Ely–Downham road, passing the Weary Travellers and Prince of Wales inns, and again paralleled by the canal it continued to Boyce's Bridge depôt.

From Boyce's Bridge the tramway was laid over private right-of-way behind an orchard to Outwell Basin station. Leaving this station the tramway encountered a short gradient, after which it crossed the Wisbech Canal by means of a steel girder bridge, supported on cast iron pillars. This had gates at the ends, so as to prevent its use as a footbridge by pedestrians anxious to make a short-cut. Crossing this bridge, the tramway crossed the road once more in order to regain the canal bank and, reaching the centre of Outwell, it crossed the waterway by a further identical bridge before entering Outwell station where a wharf was provided, with chutes for rail-barge transfers. Leaving Outwell, the tramway was laid alongside the canal (now the Old Nene) for a short distance until it reached its own right-of-way over which it continued to Upwell station. The maximum gradient was 1 in 32.

Station buildings

1. *Wisbech*

    A platform of suitable low height for the tramway type vehicles was provided at Wisbech (G.E.R.) station.

2. *Elm Bridge*

    Here there was a brick office and an open-fronted waiting room, built of wood.

3. *Boyce's Bridge*

    A small brick office building which is stated to have included accommodation for passengers.

4. *Outwell Basin*

    Here a brick office building was augmented by the provision of an old saloon coach body which served as a waiting room.

5. *Outwell*

    Facilities similar to Boyce's Bridge were established here although it is believed that in addition the ticket counter opened on to the village street.

6. *Upwell*

    The accommodation here was quite extensive; in fact it was approaching the status of a main-line station insofar as its facilities were concerned. There was a large goods yard, brick-built passenger station, and office accommodation.

7. *Other buildings*

The engine shed with two roads was adjacent to Wisbech (G.E.R.) station. There were a number of intermediate stopping places where trains called as required.

The normal daily passenger service consisted of seven or eight passenger trains each way, and on the trains, tickets were issued and collected by travelling conductors. The normal daily freight service was five freight trains per day in each direction, but this service was considerably augmented during the fruit-picking season when fruit was forwarded by both freight and passenger trains. Fruit, the principal commodity conveyed on the tramway, was conveyed in standard railway vans and wagons, although at one time special fruit vans formerly used by the G.E.R. were in use.

A competing bus service commenced on 20th May, 1920, when the Eastern Counties Road Car Company Ltd. introduced a bus service between Wisbech and Three Holes following the same route as the tramway. The bus service was extended to Welney on 9th June, 1921, and given service numbers 21 and 21A, but the whole service was discontinued on 29th June, 1922. There was a short interval when the tramway had matters to itself, but in October, 1922, a Mr. Robb of Outwell re-introduced the service between Wisbech and Three Holes.

Another independent operator came on the service when in March, 1927, a Mr. Washington of Littleport commenced a Monday and Saturday service between Wisbech and Three Holes.

The present Eastern Counties Omnibus Company service 360 between Wisbech, Welney and Ely results from the introduction in July, 1928, by the Peterborough Electric Traction Company of a daily service (numbered 60) between Wisbech and Three Holes, which service was extended to Welney in July, 1928. The business of Robb of Outwell was purchased by the Peterborough company in October, 1928.

The passenger service on the tramway ceased after 1st January, 1928, and as this book is concerned with passenger transport this is where the history really ends. However, it is worth mentioning that since 1928 the freight services decreased, except during the fruit-picking season when a considerable quantity of freight traffic still passed over the tramway. In 1961 the British Transport Commission (who at that time were the owners of the tramway, which is now owned by the British Railways Board) proposed the tramway's final closure, but such was the opposition from the fruit growers that the closure was, for the time being at any rate, not carried out. However, the axe has now fallen, the last train running on 21st May, 1966.

Motive Power
Steam Locomotives
0-4-0T, G.E.R. Nos. 125-134, Class G15:
125 built 1891 ; 126 in 1892 ; 127, 128, 130, 131, 132 in 1883 ; 129 in 1885 ; and 133, 134 in 1897. Of these numbers 125, 126, 130, 131, 133 and 134 are known to have worked on the Wisbech and Upwell.

These locomotives were introduced by T. W. Worsdell (Locomotive Superintendent of the G.E.R., 1881-1885) and weighed 21 tons 5 cwt. in working order. These engines had cow-catchers, warning bells, and governors which shut off steam and applied the brakes if a speed of 10 m.p.h. was exceeded. The entire engine, which could be driven from either end, was enclosed in a wooden casing and had the appearance of a freight brake van. This structure had a large cast number plate on each side and was fitted with movable glazed windows in the ends. The motion was concealed behind metal skirting. Some of these first ten engines survived the grouping and became L.N.E.R. class Y6.

Between 1903 and 1921 a number of these original 0-4-0T locomotives were replaced by powerful 0-6-0T fully-enclosed 27-ton tramway locomotives (G.E.R. class C53), designed by Holden (Locomotive Superintendent of the G.E.R., 1885-1907). In certain cases these locomotives took the numbers of the earlier locomotives which in turn had their numbers prefixed by '0'. The new additions had the same general appearance as the 0-4-0T locomotives with boarding between the cabs and skirting below the frames.

Numbers 125, 126 and 129 were built in 1921 ; 127, 128 and 131 in 1921 ; 130 in 1910 ; 135, 136 in 1903 ; and 137, 138, 139 in 1908. Of these 128, 130, 131, 136 and 137 are known to have worked on the tramway. Some of the locomotives were used on the quayside lines at Yarmouth and Ipswich.

In 1939 two Sentinel geared locomotives were put to work on the tramway. They had 0-4-0 wheel arrangement, were of 200 h.p., and weighed 24 tons. They were given L.N.E.R. numbers 8403 and 8404. Later they were transferred to work on the quay tramways. Further progressive dieselisation led to the withdrawal of the last steam locomotive in August, 1955. The Drewry diesel locomotives latterly in use on the tramway had fully-enclosed motion and a special warning bell mounted on top of the casing.

184

A latter-day scene on the Wisbech and Upwell tramway; Drewry 200 h.p. diesel shunting locomotive with freight train at Elm Bridge depôt.

Photo: British Railways Board

Rolling Stock

Passenger vehicles were of two types, viz.:

(a) *Tramway-type bogie vehicles with open end platforms*

These vehicles were 37 ft. in length overall, and 8 ft. 4 in. wide overall. The bodies were mounted on bogies of 4 ft. 6 in. wheelbase at 17 ft. 6 in. centres. Entrance was by means of a platform at each end of the body; the platforms each carried a set of graduated steps at each side. The buffer beam was divided in the centre to facilitate a gangway from one coach to the next, and each end platform was provided with an ornamental railing which had a hinged centre section giving access to the connecting gangway. Gates of similar design extended between this railing and the body. By locking certain gates it was possible to limit access to certain platforms. Longitudinal seating and gas lighting were provided in each vehicle.

A number of these coaches were transferred to the Kelvedon and Tollesbury Light Railway and one of them, since scrapped, was featured in the film "The Titfield Thunderbolt" made during the early 1950s.

(b) *Four-wheel vehicles*

A similar design of four-wheel coach was also in use but these had 12 windows per side as opposed to the 19 windows per side of the bogie coaches.

The late Dr. Whitcombe states that there were nine passenger coaches.

In addition to the freight and passenger stock there was a travelling office which was in use for many years on freight trains.

There was a proposal to extend the tramway to Wisbech (Market Place) and also onwards from Upwell to Three Holes Bridge. In addition there was a proposal to construct another tramway from Wisbech (G.E.R.) to Terrington Station on the Midland and Great Northern Railway.

Specimen ticket of the Wisbech and Upwell steam tramway.

Specimen tickets of the Kelvedon and Tollesbury Light Railway.

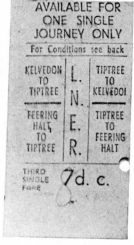

186

OTHER LIGHT RAILWAYS

Although really outside the scope of this book, a brief note on the light railways which flourished in East Anglia is not out of place. The general features are set out below and any reader who wishes to obtain full details of these undertakings is recommended to the publications mentioned in the bibliography.

Kelvedon and Tollesbury Light Railway

As with the Southwold Railway (below) this railway has been dealt with in book form ('The Kelvedon and Tollesbury Light Railway'— published by Branchline Handbooks) and for this reason only a brief description is included here.

This light railway was constructed under the provisions of the Light Railways Acts, 1896 and 1901, which offered the benefits of cheap construction and economical methods of working. Owned by the Great Eastern Railway (who promoted the Light Railway) the railway ran

A train on the Kelvedon and Tollesbury Light Railway in 1910.
Photo: K. A. C. R. Nunn

187

from its own station at Kelvedon, on the Colchester main line, through the fruit-growing area of Essex to Tiptree and on to the coast at Tollesbury where a timber pier was constructed.

The railway was laid to the standard gauge of 4 ft. 8½ in. and was opened from Kelvedon to Tollesbury on 1st October, 1904, and on to Tollesbury Pier on 15th May, 1907. The mileage was 9.90 miles.

Originally, open saloon cars of tramway type were used for passenger traffic, but latterly lightweight bogie coaches (ex-Wisbech and Upwell) and standard four-wheel coaches with partitions removed were used for this purpose. Motive power was provided by a J67 0-6-0T locomotive.

In 1923, when the railway companies were grouped, the Kelvedon and Tollesbury Light Railway became part of the London and North Eastern Railway which was nationalised in 1947, becoming the Eastern Region of British Railways.

The portion beyond Tollesbury station to the coast was taken over during the 1939–45 war by the War Department and four locomotives worked on the light railway hauling mobile guns; the track on the pier at Tollesbury was lifted and removed during 1940.

A twice-daily passenger train service operated between Kelvedon and Tollesbury and vice versa, at one time onto the timber pier at Tollesbury. The line, which is now closed to all traffic, was closed to passenger traffic on 5th May, 1951.

Southwold Railway

In view of the fact that a book ('The Southwold Railway' by E. S. Tonks) has already been published about this railway only a brief history setting out the main details is included here.

The Southwold Railway was constructed under its own Act of Parliament of 1876 and was opened for passenger and freight traffic on 24th September, 1879, but after 1879 it was worked as a Light Railway under the Regulation of Railways Act, 1868. The undertaking was operated by the Southwold Railway Company, which had been incorporated by the Act of 1876. The rails, laid to a track gauge of 3 ft., were flat bottomed, weighed 30 lb. to the yard and were spiked to wood sleepers. Messrs. Ransomes and Rapier of Ipswich were the contractors who built the railway.

Locomotive and train on the Southwold Railway at Halesworth.
Photo: Kingsway Real Photo Series

The Station, Blythburgh.

A Southwold Railway mixed train at Blythburgh.

Between Southwold and Halesworth—a distance of 8¾ miles—
stations were situated at Walberswick, Blythburgh, and Wenhaston.
The only addition made to the route mileage during the railway's
existence was a branch opened in 1915 to Southwold Harbour. This
branch, however, was little used and soon fell into disuse. The major
engineering works along the line of route were a swing bridge over
the River Blyth at Southwold and a substantial overbridge over a road
at Halesworth.

Three Sharp Stewart 2-4-0T locomotives were delivered for the
opening of the railway and were numbered and named as follows:

> No. 1—"Southwold" (Returned to manufacturers, 1883)
> No. 2—"Halesworth"
> No. 3—"Blyth"

Passenger rolling stock consisted of six six-wheel Cleminson flexible-
wheelbase tramway-type saloon coaches which, it is thought, were
originally built for the Woosung Tramroad, China, but not delivered.
Each coach had longitudinal seating; the seats in the third-class compartments (there were four third-class coaches and two first/third-class
coaches) were covered with a strip of carpet, but those in the first-class
compartments had blue cushions. Entrance was by means of open
platforms at the ends of the coaches; interior lighting was provided
by oil lamps. During the winter the floors were covered with straw as
there was no train heating. Rolling stock available for the conveyance
of freight traffic consisted of two four-wheel luggage vans, 21 four-
wheel wagons, and six six-wheel wagons—three of which had been
purchased second-hand from Thomas Moy Limited who owned five
wagons.

Originally the locomotives were finished in a green livery, but later
Great Eastern Railway blue with red lining was introduced. Coaches
were originally cream with black lining and lettering, then cream with
black lettering (no lining) and finally maroon with black (later white)
lettering. Wagons were painted grey with white lettering.

Most trains were made up of both passenger and freight vehicles,
and train working was by staff and telegraph with slotted semaphore
home and starting signals on a common post at each station. The
maximum permitted speed of trains was 16 miles per hour. There was
no continuous brake, and handbrakes were provided only on the locomotives and three of the coaches.

In 1883 locomotive No. 1, "Southwold," was returned to Messrs. Sharp Stewart as there was not enough work for three locomotives, but by 1893 traffic had considerably increased and another locomotive was purchased. This locomotive, which was a Sharp Stewart 2-4-2T, was given the number 1 and named "Southwold." The railway became quite busy during the early 1900s, and in 1914, shortly after the branch to Southwold Harbour had been opened, a fourth locomotive was purchased for the expected increase in traffic. This time a different manufacturer was chosen—Manning, Wardle—and the 0-6-2T locomotive they built for the railway became No. 4, "Wenhaston."

With the development after the First World War of road traffic for passengers and freight, traffic on the railway declined, and as a result the railway was closed to all traffic on 11th April, 1929, giving the Southwold Railway the rather unfortunate distinction of being the first of the public passenger-carrying narrow-gauge railways to cease operating.

After the closure, the only locomotive to be immediately scrapped was the 2-4-2T No. 1 "Southwold," which was scrapped during May, 1929.

A rather curious feature of the railway was that after closure the locomotives stood in the sheds and the rolling stock stood on the sidings steadily deteriorating until 1942 when the railway was demolished during a war-time scrap metal drive. It was at this time that the bridge over the River Blyth at Southwold was blown up.

The railway has been in the news fairly recently (1961) when the road overbridge at Halesworth was removed. It is interesting that the railway still retains a legal existence, as an Act of Parliament is required to abandon the line.

In 1899 it was proposed to construct a 12¼-mile standard-gauge line from Southwold to Lowestoft, and an application was submitted to the Light Railway Commissioners in May, 1899, but was withdrawn before reaching the stage of a local enquiry. This scheme was replaced by an amended application which was submitted for a Light Railway Order to convert the existing line to 4 ft. 8½ in. gauge and work it under the Light Railways Act, 1896. A further proposal contained in this application was to construct a 9-mile standard-gauge line from Southwold to Kessingland, where it would have joined the Great Eastern Railway's authorised branch from Lowestoft to Kessingland.

An enquiry was held at Southwold on 18th December, 1900, by the Light Railway Commissioners, who approved the proposal and sent it to the Board of Trade on 23rd July, 1901. At the Board of Trade hearing on 17th October, 1901, the National Electric Traction Company Limited objected on the grounds that the Southwold Railway Company was authorised to build its line across a road in Kessingland, with a proviso that this part should not be built except to make a junction with the proposed Great Eastern Railway branch line. At this time the National Electric Traction Company had an Order (East Anglian Light Railway Company—see Chapter 5) before the Board of Trade for confirmation for a line along this road. As it was a late objection, the Chairman would consider it only in regard to public safety, but in the end the Committee allowed the level crossing to remain. As a result the Order was confirmed on 4th April, 1902, but it is stated that the Southwold Railway Company could not raise the necessary capital (£84,249) and nothing came of the proposal.

Specimen tickets of the Southwold Railway.

CHAPTER EIGHT

PROPOSED TRAMWAYS and LIGHT RAILWAYS

IN many of the towns in East Anglia where tramway systems were constructed, several rival schemes were considered before the final proposals were formulated and, where applicable, these schemes are mentioned in the chapter dealing with the individual city or town concerned.

However, there were a number of proposed schemes for tramways and light railways which did not, in the event, reach the stage of construction, and it is interesting that they were mainly of an interurban character. It is a summary of these schemes which forms the subject of this chapter.

Clacton-on-Sea and St. Osyth Light Railway Company

This was one of the exceptions insofar as track gauge was concerned (the other known proposed exception was the Warboys and Puddock Drove Tramway, see below). This tramway, which was promoted in 1901, was to have been 4.49 miles in length, laid to a track gauge of 4 ft. 8½ in. The route was to have been from the Pier Head (Clacton-on-Sea) via Clacton-on-Sea, Great Clacton, and Coppens Green to St. Osyth.

Although permission was received in 1904 for construction of the tramway, no further development was undertaken.

Terrington and Walpole Tramroads

This was to have been a 4 ft. 8½ in. gauge steam tramway from Terrington Midland and Great Northern Railway station to Walpole Highway. The tramway was to have been on private right-of-way from Terrington to Shipley Gate Green and from St. John's Highway to Walpole Highway. Between Shipley Gate and St. John's Highway it was to have been on a roadside reservation.

193

The plans were deposited on 16th November, 1888, for the 1889 session, and this application was granted by the Terrington and Walpole Tramroads Company Act of 1889. On 19th November, 1889, further proposals were deposited to be considered during the 1890 session. These proposals were known as the "Terrington and Walpole Tramroads Company, Extension to Wisbech" and featured a private right-of-way tramway from Walpole Highway via West Walton to Wisbech (G.E.R.). Nothing, however, came of either scheme.

Oakington and Cottenham Light Railway

The application by Power and Traction Limited was heard at Cambridge on 27th January, 1900, for a Light Railway Order for a line from Oakington station goods yard on the Cambridge and St. Ives line of the G.E.R., passing through Cottenham to a point near the Cottenham Canal, with a short branch from Cottenham westwards to some brickfields. It was to be partly on land to be acquired, partly on roadside waste, and partly on the public road. The total length was to be four miles and the gauge 2 ft. 6 in. Steam motive power was to have been used. Standard-gauge goods wagons were to have been carried on the line by transporter cars.

While not lodging objections to the proposed line, certain landowners asked for provisions minimising the risk of, and making the company liable for, all damage arising from fires caused by sparks from the engines, and they pointed out the very narrow strip of land it would occupy. The promoters asked that where the line was on roadside verge and where crossings into fields had to be provided, then these sections of line should not require to be metalled, but timber should be used instead. Cottenham Parish Council asked for morning and evening workpeople's cars for the conveyance of fruit pickers.

The Light Railway Commissioners granted the Order, with no special provision regarding sparks and fire, but field entrances were to be metalled. The Order also provided for a cheap train each way each weekday, morning and evening, to be operated before 7 a.m. and after 5.30 p.m. Fares were to be charged at not more than ½d. per mile. The Commissioners gave the Cambridgeshire County Council power to purchase after 40 years, at fair market value.

The Order was submitted to the Board of Trade on 16th July, 1900, and confirmed on 25th January, 1901. The Board of Trade added a clause that where the line was on roadside verges there was to be at least 18 feet of roadway (metalled or unmetalled) between the nearest rail and the opposite edge of the road or, if there was to be a footpath on the opposite side of the road, the outside of the footpath. However, no construction was undertaken on the line, which would have been 3 miles, 7 furlongs, and 4.5 chains in length.

Harwich Electric Lighting and Tramways Co. Ltd.

This was a proposed combined scheme suggested in 1899 for the introduction in Harwich of tramways and electric lighting. Nothing, however, came of the proposal.

Walton-on-the-Naze and Frinton Tramway

Authorised by the Walton-on-the-Naze and Frinton Improvements Act 1879, this was to have been a standard-gauge horse tramway of 2.34 miles between the above-mentioned points via Frinton railway station (Great Eastern Railway). The promoters were the Walton-on-the-Naze and Frinton Improvements Company.

Southwold and Halesworth Tramway

Authorised in 1872, under the Tramways Orders Confirmation (No. 3) Act, this proposed steam tramway scheme fell through for lack of funds. The promoters were the Lowestoft, Yarmouth and Southwold Tramways Company Ltd.

Warboys and Puddock Drove Tramway

This proposed standard-gauge tramway was to have run from Warboys railway station in a dead straight line of single track with passing loops for 4.10 miles to the Huntingdonshire county boundary. Animal, steam or electric power was suggested, and plans were deposited on 20th November, 1889, for the 1890 Parliamentary Session, but nothing came of the scheme.

BIBLIOGRAPHY

'A Detailed History of the fleet of Eastern Counties Omnibus Company Limited and of the fleets of the Corporations of Great Yarmouth, Ipswich and Lowestoft.' Published by the P.S.V. Circle/ Omnibus Society.

'A.B.C. of Narrow Gauge Railways,' by W. J. K. Davies.

'British Bus Fleets, East Anglia.'

'Buses Illustrated.' Published by Ian Allan Ltd.

Coast Development Corporation file. Company file at the Public Record Office.

'The Conurbations of Great Britain,' by T. W. Freeman.

'Eastern Daily Press.' Various editions.

'Eastern Evening News.' Various editions.

'Eastern Electricity,' November, 1960. Magazine of the Eastern Electricity Board.

'Essex Life,' November, 1963.

'Golden Age of Tramways,' by C. F. Klapper.

'Great British Tramway Networks,' by W. H. Bett and J. C. Gillham. Published by the Light Railway Transport League.

'Great Eastern Railway,' by Cecil J. Allen, M.Inst.T., A.I.Loco.E.

'History, Gazetteer and Directory of Norfolk, 1890.' Published by William White Ltd.

'The Kelvedon and Tollesbury Light Railway,' by N. J. Stapleton.

'Modern Tramway.' Periodical published by the Light Railway Transport League.

'Modern Transport.' Periodical.

'Narrow Gauge Album,' by P. B. Whitehouse.

'Norwich Electric Tramways Company—Rule Book for Employees.'

'Norwich Electric Tramways, Souvenir Booklet, 1960.' Published by the Tramway and Omnibus Historical Society, Norwich.

'Old Motor.' Periodical.

'Passenger Transport.' Periodical.

'Railway Magazine.' Periodical. September, 1923; June, 1952.

'The Southern Omnibus Review—Colchester Corporation.'

'Some Account of the Wisbech and Upwell Tramway from 1882 till Today.' Technical Course "A," Isle of Ely College, July, 1958.

'Southwold Railway,' by E. S. Tonks.

'Tramway and Railway World' (now 'Transport World'). Periodical.

'Tramway Society Bulletin.' Article by H. V. Jinks, 'The Norwich Aerodrome Extension,' November, 1959. Published by the Tramway and Light Railway Society.

'Tramways of East Anglia.' Paper by Gordon Taylor, 1950. Published by the Light Railway Transport League.